Ideas Exchange

Ideas Exchange
The Collaborative Studio of Hawkins\Brown

Tim Abrahams

Birkhäuser
Basel

Layout: Karen Willcox, www.aleatoria.com, Winchester
Reprographics: DawkinsColour, London

Library of Congress Control Number: 2010927347

Bibliographic information published by the German National Library
The German National Library lists this publication in the Deutsche
Nationalbibliografie; detailed bibliographic data are available on the
Internet at http://dnb.d-nb.de.

© 2010 Birkhäuser GmbH
Basel
P.O. Box 133, CH-4010 Basel, Switzerland

Printed on acid-free paper produced from chlorine-free pulp. TCF ∞
Printed in Germany
ISBN: 978-3-0346-0231-0

9 8 7 6 5 4 3 2 1

www.birkhauser-architecture.com

Acknowledgements

Our thanks and gratitude are extended to the following people

Henriette Mueller-Stahl
Michael Wachholz

Lucy Dinnen
Alex Smith

Karen Willcox

Tim Abrahams

Lee Mallett

Jes Fernie
Adam Hart
Vicky Richardson
Adam Ritchie
Erik Spiekermann

John Simpson

Very special thanks to everyone who has worked for Hawkins\
Brown in the past and to all our clients, co-workers, consultants,
contractors and collaborators, in fact everyone and anyone who
has helped to make our architecture of the last 21 years.

Hawkins\Brown's roots go back more than 20 years, to the late 1980s, an era that economically was characterised by a distinct recession. The architects who set out their stall in those stormy times, such as AHMM, Caruso St John Architects, Foreign Office Architects for example, have tangibly different characteristics from the group which had opened their practices in the Thatcherite boom of the 1980s, like John McAslan & Partners, Allies & Morrison, or ORMS.

That earlier generation reacted to Prince Charles' very public anti-modernist tirade delivered at their profession's 150th anniversary in 1983 in a complex way. They smarted from it, but yet they also appeared embarrassed by the immodesty of the postmodernist movement and its widespread dilution into a pastiche that was frequently used to sidestep aesthetic arguments and win planning consent. They strove to re-assert something of the modernist 'auteur' status of the architect.

While these earlier 'neo-moderns' of the mid-1980s are now into their mature phase, slightly younger practices, like Hawkins\Brown, are only just beginning to win commissions to design big, complex buildings and convince clients and users with their own agenda. I would argue their design priorities and aesthetic and constructional innovations are derived from and driven by the deprivations of the 1990s recession. They also spring from an awareness of the inadequacies of modernist urban design and the inflexibility of its architecture. Whilst they had their roots in the radical economic circumstances architects found themselves in, during the early part of the decade, they strengthened in response to the demands for 'green' building which became widespread as the 1990s progressed. Architects are now well prepared for the beginning of the 21st century.

Hawkins\Brown's approach can be characterised by a willingness to explore different aesthetics, materials and forms. They embrace community engagements and collaborations with other creative contributors. Architects, they suggest, are no longer the lone directors of their art and instead have learned to be team players in a much more comprehensive way than in the recent past.

The contemporary emphasis on sustainability reinforces this approach. Implicit is a more 'caring' attitude. Investors and occupiers demand that their buildings deliver Corporate Social Responsibility pledges, whether they are an expression of genuinely held beliefs or politically correct expedients. But it is the harsh lessons of recession which scar deepest and arguably produce the more creative, leaner and longer-lasting architectural practices, in terms of both design and business.

Unlike the 1980s which was typified by cultural rift, the 1990s released a wider range of architectural responses. The flowery shirts sported by the directors of Hawkins\Brown were perhaps a symbol of this new, softer, broader palette which began to open up. In Hawkins\Brown's work from this era – most of it situated in London – these traits were revealed in the early and inexpensive new-build Playbarn project in Newham (1989) and in the re-use of Bradbury Street workshops (early 1990s) in Hackney, and the creation of the small, but iconic 'urban souk' market stalls (1997) which helped kick-start new economic activity in a rundown East End locale. The long-standing relationship with this part of Hackney is also evidence of Hawkins\Brown's commitment to and empathy with the notion of community.

The self-awareness of architects that resulted from that era now prompts the thought that perhaps gratuitous form-making can seem self-serving or superficial, while attachment to a signature style no longer seems relevant given the changed set of circumstances architects are confronted with – another difference between this generation and its immediate predecessors. The lust for the 'iconic' may be spent, for a while at least, and in its place a growing enthusiasm for more apposite and sensitive responses has arisen. Roger Hawkins, Russell Brown and David Bickle are reflecting the social agenda. And maybe this has made architecture rather more like art practice, not less. David Bickle in particular feels affinity with art practice and the way it can empower architecture, while Russell Brown's extrovert communication skills articulate the practice's architectural ideas particularly effectively. Roger Hawkins' political nous and determined delivery of projects add the steely will required to get architecture built.

Collectively they recognise there is a need to interrogate the programme of a building more rigorously today. It is too restrictive to impose a form on a programme, the culture of

which might change rapidly in the not-too-distant future. Even lawyers have now eschewed individual offices and mingle with their peers in a collaborative Bürolandschaft workspace. If lawyers can do it, perhaps a 'culture change' could be part of a better solution.

Perhaps, as the directors of Hawkins\Brown suggest, changes in the educational sector have informed other types of building. The need to make spaces that encourage the exchange of ideas stems from the organisational configurations required by education. This is also an architectural programme desired by businesses seeking to attract and retain staff and to energise the dormant creativity in their enterprises – a transformation that is often an urgent matter of survival – evolve or die. It is architecture which can make survival and growth possible.

This is not as easy as it sounds. Tottenham Court Road Crossrail interchange has been hugely influential in the life of the practice, which was originally picked for the job 20 years ago. They were chosen because of their obvious promise and because they would still be working when the project would finally be completed. This was a project which required working imaginatively and resourcefully with an existing 'building', albeit underground. It has also been an eminently collaborative undertaking between engineers, artists, railwaymen and changing client bodies, requiring constant review and accommodation of change. Although it is a fascinating combination of collaborations with artists and engineers, it is still impossible to think of it as a typical project. There is no such thing for Hawkins\Brown.

Yet it does reveal that it is so necessary for architectural practices like Hawkins\Brown to be committed to social and economic engagement – to collaboration in response to the turmoil of changing ideas, technology, and economic circumstances. This generation of architects understands the adage that the only constant is change, and that it requires ingenuity, flexibility, determination, but above all a willingness to look beyond the closeted environment of the studio, to make buildings which can truly address such a transformative era as we are currently experiencing.

April 2010
Lee Mallett

Opposite Highfields
Automotive &
Engineering Training
Centre, Nottingham.

012\
Collaborating
with
Architects

Twice as Nice
by Vicky Richardson

For the first time in 2008 a collective of architects, rather than a single designer, was named winner of the UK's most important architectural award, the Stirling Prize for the Accordia housing complex in Cambridge. The idea of architects collaborating on an equal footing with their peers seems rather new and even risqué compared with the system that dominates the international competitions to select the architects for significant buildings, where the same list of stars compete in a 'no-holds-barred' battle of the egos.

Although the collaborative approach on Accordia was not prompted by economic concerns, its timing is interesting. In a recession, so the thinking goes, architects are more likely to co-operate out of necessity. The possible backlash against iconic buildings following the economic downturn is beginning to establish a cultural climate that favours more modest architectural statements. Instead of a scenario where the reputation of a single designer is as important as the design itself, the argument is that a response from a group of designers can offer a more balanced and rounded architecture.

Christoph Egret of Studio Egret West, with whom Hawkins\Brown have collaborated on a number of projects, argues that the age of the "ego-architect is on the wane", and that collaborations between like-minded practices are the way forward. "The big names are less important. I feel that I'm surrounded by practices that are happy to stay small. When you grow large, you become a dinosaur that just needs to be fed with work." Collaborating with architects improves the end product and, almost more importantly, is a way of honing an architectural approach. "You get really good self-criticism, which you don't get with clients. Clients are usually concerned with the commercial impact of the design, but with architects you get wonderful conversations about the approach and use of materials that make the outcome of the project better."

Is this vision of a new era of collaborative working realistic? Certainly, in recent years the perception has been of architects competing within limited groups of practices specialising in a certain type of work. In this scenario practices have sought to emphasise their differences rather than their collective interests. The economic boom, and the rush to take advantage of development opportunities in the Middle East and East Asia, have fuelled competition and individualisation. At the same time, the collapse of cohering movements in architecture has contributed to a sense of fragmentation within the profession.

This emphasis on individuality and originality begins from the moment an undergraduate leaves architecture school and seeks his or her first job in an architects office. Since the 1960s the number of students in higher education has quadrupled. Under the New Labour government, over the decade of the 1990s, the increase was particularly dramatic. In the early 1990s a typical year group in an architecture school was made up of 30 undergraduates. Today it is more likely to be 150. Many of those students are destined never to work as 'traditional' architects, yet it seems likely that the trend will continue towards specialisation and fragmentation within the profession.

Against this backdrop of professional tribalism, where many firms spend a great deal of time and money on marketing and graphic identity to differentiate themselves, collaboration can appear to be a new and progressive concept.

Perhaps we are entering a golden era of collaboration. During the 1980s, the architect became increasingly just a member of the construction team, rather than the leader of it, a trend which led to a great deal of frustration for clients as well as architects. In many ways the Latham Report of 1994 went some way to resolving these contractual confusions. This influential report sought clarification of the relationships in the construction industry. It argued that the construction process should rely on a set of basic principles; that there should be a complete family of interlocking contractual documents and that adjudication should be the normal form of dispute resolution. The report became the basis for increased 'partnering' between architects and other consultants, even if the architect's role as head of the design team was diminished through the increasing emphasis on design/build forms of contract.

The advent of partnering and commitment to 'teamworking' across the construction team may have encouraged collaboration by years of criticism, but the confidence of the

architectural profession itself had been undermined. The post-war rebuilding programme of the 1950s had placed architects in a strong position and allowed them to pass on work and commissions to younger talent. Many architects' reputations were established not just as designers, but also as commissioners and clients. At the young age of 38, Hugh Casson was appointed as Director of Architecture for the Festival of Britain. The position enabled him to give work to his peers and to young architects including Powell and Moya, Wells Coates, and Leslie Martin. Martin was Casson's most important appointments. He had already worked as deputy architect of London County Council (LCC) during the Second World War, and for the festival he was chosen to lead a team of architects to design the Royal Festival Hall.

With plenty of work to go around, and by today's standards, a relatively small number of architects, it was easier for the profession to be constituted as a series of 'families' that supported each other. After building the Festival Hall, Martin went on to become chief architect of the LCC, where he in turn was able to sponsor young talent like Patrick Hodgkinson, the Smithsons, Colin St John Wilson, and James Stirling, who were all commissioned to design housing in the capital early on in their careers.

In 1957 nearly half of all British architects were directly employed by the public sector, most of them in local authorities. The majority of county councils had their own architects' departments headed up by a Chief Architect. Often the role of the Chief Architect was to bring in specialist private firms to collaborate where they had a particular expertise. In the 1950s Sheppard Robson, YRM, and Architects Co-Partnerships specialised in building schools. London authorities, who had large in-house teams, worked with independent architects who brought in radical new ideas: Westminster brought in Powell and Moya; the Borough of Finsbury worked with Tecton; and Hackney with Frederick Gibberd.

Lewis Womersley, the Chief Architect of Sheffield City Council, sought the new ideas of Ivor Smith and Jack Lynn to create the world-famous housing megastructure at Parkhill. Hawkins\Brown in turn have benefitted from this gesture, being picked by Urban Splash as young talents to redevelop the scheme 40 years later.

Without the important role of the public sector architects department and the chief architect, this informal support between architects has broken down. It is still possible to point to some practices that support former employees but only as long as they do not offer serious commercial competition. Generally the sense of the profession as made up of family networks of architects has passed. Collaboration, then, is far from being a fashionable new concept. Throughout the 20th century, on large or complex projects, it was the norm rather than the exception, and often created an environment for greater innovation with the design.

If we go right back to the beginnings of the profession of architecture we can see that collaboration was one of its underlying principles. Until 1847, the culture of master/pupil meant that established architects passed on work to young talent, a practice that was part and parcel of the system of training for architects. The creation of the first British school of architecture, the Architectural Association, was the beginning of a process that has seen a gradual move away from the pupilage system to one that is now solely based in academic institutions. This shift has led to significant changes in the way that architects influence and shape future generations of architects, and in the overall coherence of the profession.

Even the greatest architects have accepted that a good building might need a team that includes more than one architectural approach. In the 1920s, Sir Edwin Lutyens collaborated with other firms on designs for offices in the City of London: on the Midland Bank in Poultry Street (1924–26), Lutyens took care of the overall design, drawings for the elevations, roof, ground floor and fifth floor board room. Gotch & Saunders designed everything else. For the Manchester Midland Bank, he worked in partnership with Whinney, Son & Austin Hall in 1929.

In the USA, the division between design architect and executive architect has been established for some years. This means that collaboration between firms is a widely established practice.

In Japan, the system of 'sempai' (senior), where a young architect has to work for a master for several years before setting up on his own, is becoming less common. While in the past it was practically impossible for outsiders to get work, now there are several high-profile emerging practices that have bypassed the established practices. Takero Shimazaki, who worked for several years in the Tokyo studio of Itsuko Hasegawa, says: "Toyo Ito, the sort of head of the Japanese architecture profession, is beginning to change the system and now more architects, such as Sou Fujimoto and Terunobu Fujimori, are breaking the mould. Only Tadao Ando still really pushes for sempai – he likes architects to stay with him for 4–5 years."

In Europe, partnerships between international design architects and native firms

Opposite A silk model of Parkhill was exhibited in the British Pavilion as part of the Venice Architecture Biennale in 2006.

are routine as a means to negotiate complicated and locally specific building codes. The Norwegian practice Snøhetta, which is working on high-profile projects all over the world, recognises that local partnerships provide an important source of information. For the Margate Turner Centre competition, it teamed up with Stephen Spence to form Snøhetta Spence. The team won the competition, although the scheme fell victim to local politics and was dropped. David Chipperfield, the architect who took over the project, works in a similar way, selecting local architects to complete designs in Alaska, Venice or Berlin.

Russell Brown is enthusiastic about the practices' collaborative work but this is tempered with some practical considerations: "Any risk-averse client is worried about how they control the creative energies of their architects. If there are more architects then this risk increases. For each of our collaborations contractual responsibilities have to be made very clear."

There is no doubt that a common ethos is the most successful basis for a working relationship and that more than one architect on a project can make a better building. But collaborations are always in flux. A common scenario is of architects joining together to enter a competition at a time when the deadlines and the enthusiasm for the design overcome any misgivings. The architects are then forced to revaluate the relationship if they win the project. Partnerships with other architects tend to be more fluid in the UK, part of what makes them potentially creative and interesting.

The London-based practice Toh Shimazaki Architecture achieved its earliest commissions through the support of Richard Rogers Partnership, for which Toh had worked, but also by collaborating with large firms that were very different, such as Assael Architecture, Nightingale Associates and BDP. Shimazaki is positive about the experience, but admits that this sort of business relationship can be difficult. In his eyes, "it is advantageous when architects bring different characters to a project and have different aims, but keeping down the urge to compete requires a lot of self-discipline."

Hawkins\Brown have had the same experience looking to work with smaller practices with different skills or more commercial practices who are happy to follow their design lead.

Collaboration can often be a means by which established practices maintain a studio culture in their offices, where design decisions are interrogated and young talented architects are motivated. Opening up the process to outside architects whom a practice respects can re-create the atmosphere and creativity of an architecture school. The culture of the 'crit', where a group of architects from different backgrounds gather together to present and criticise an emerging scheme, is something that most practices could benefit from, though few are brave enough to open their office to such scrutiny.

Despite the forces pulling them apart, architects have an urge to stick together: why else would London's Clerkenwell have the highest concentration of practices in the UK, with around 2,000 working within a few square miles. The recession, which began to hit architects in 2008, was hardest on those medium to large-sized firms that had grown rapidly to meet the demand for developer-led homes. One impact of this has been to reinforce the decision by a generation setting up on their own to stay small. Just as Lutyens found in the 1920s, collaboration offers a way of taking on more work, while trying to maintain design quality.

From the outset Hawkins\Brown looked to share financial risk or gain access to different markets through forming collaborations and partnerships. One of their first projects was to set up a design and build company with Jarvis Contractors and Interplay, a play equipment design firm, to create a design/build product. This developed a series of modular play buildings which could offer a 'turnkey' product to local authorities. This enabled Hawkins\Brown to win local authority work before they had three years' accounts to qualify for frameworks.

Collaborations between architects take place for a variety of reasons, and are as complex as buildings themselves. More than any legal or contractual drive to partner, the best reason to work together is often a shared aspiration, even a shared ideology. Even in the 1980s, the battle between modernism and postmodernism provided a framework within which architects could find opponents and allies. While the current profession may not have the cohering social goals of post-war modernism, differing approaches to the debate about sustainability and design for climate change are having the effect of encouraging like-minded practices to come together to bid jointly, to share resources and discuss designs. It is unlikely that this ideology will unite architects in the way that modernism did, but what is important is that this dialogue does take place and that the work that is produced is recognised for its different quality.

Opposite Parkhill, Sheffield, under construction, 2009.

020\
Parkhill, Sheffield

In 2003, Roger Hawkins and David Bickle were working together on a Maggie's Cancer Caring Centre in Sheffield, one of the series of buildings developed by Charles Jencks in memory of his wife Maggie Keswick. For Roger Hawkins it was a return to a city he knew well, having studied at the University. Like many other architects, he became fascinated with Parkhill, the huge council housing estate that, like a snake of brutalism, had been coiled around one of the hills of the city in the early 1960s. Despite the fact that it became a Grade II* listed building in 1998, Parkhill, the largest protected building in Europe, was in a deplorable state. Hawkins\Brown approached the firm Urban Splash with an idea to develop the decaying estate. Although renowned for tackling difficult sites and championing architectural causes, Urban Splash were reluctant to take on such a huge project. Six months later a competition to deliver a refurbishment of the 995-dwelling block, was advertised for developer/architect teams in the *Official Journal of the European Union (OJEU)*.

When Hawkins\Brown presented their ideas a second time to Nick Johnson of Urban Splash, they were still met with significant apprehension. In her book *Estates: An Intimate History*, Lynsey Hanley records that by 2007 in a building that was "partially empty and infested with pigeons" there was an average of only two inhabitants per apartment. Furthermore Hanley, no fan of modernist built estates, clearly found the decision to list the building questionable.

Yet others were convinced of Parkhill's architectural value. The building was completed in 1961, designed by Ivor Smith and Jack Lynn under the aegis of Lewis Wormersely, Sheffield's Chief Architect. Lynn and Smith were strongly influenced by the work of Le Corbusier, particularly his planning document *La Ville radieuse*. It was a visit to the building that won over Nick Johnson. David Bickle remembers exploring the virtues of the complex: "The dual aspect apartments with natural ventilation and daylight and panoramic views; the way the whole building responds to the topography of the site; the changes in scale of the elevations between the northern and southern courtyards. As the buildings get taller the courtyards open up, so the size of the courtyards responds to the scale of the elevations. It's an incredibly intelligent design."

The aesthetic and political charge of Parkhill is undiminished. Since they started on the project, Urban Splash and Hawkins\Brown have been severely criticised for taking on such a disregarded building. (In 2005, a Channel 4 programme asked the public which buildings they most wanted to see demolished, Parkhill made the 'final' and was voted as one of Great Britain's ugliest structures most worthy of demolition.) At the same time the developers and architects have been castigated by some conservationists for adulterating the modernist purity of the

Above Prior to regeneration, the estate is partially occupied and in a state of extreme disrepair.

Opposite Proposed masterplan illustrating re-programmed public realm.

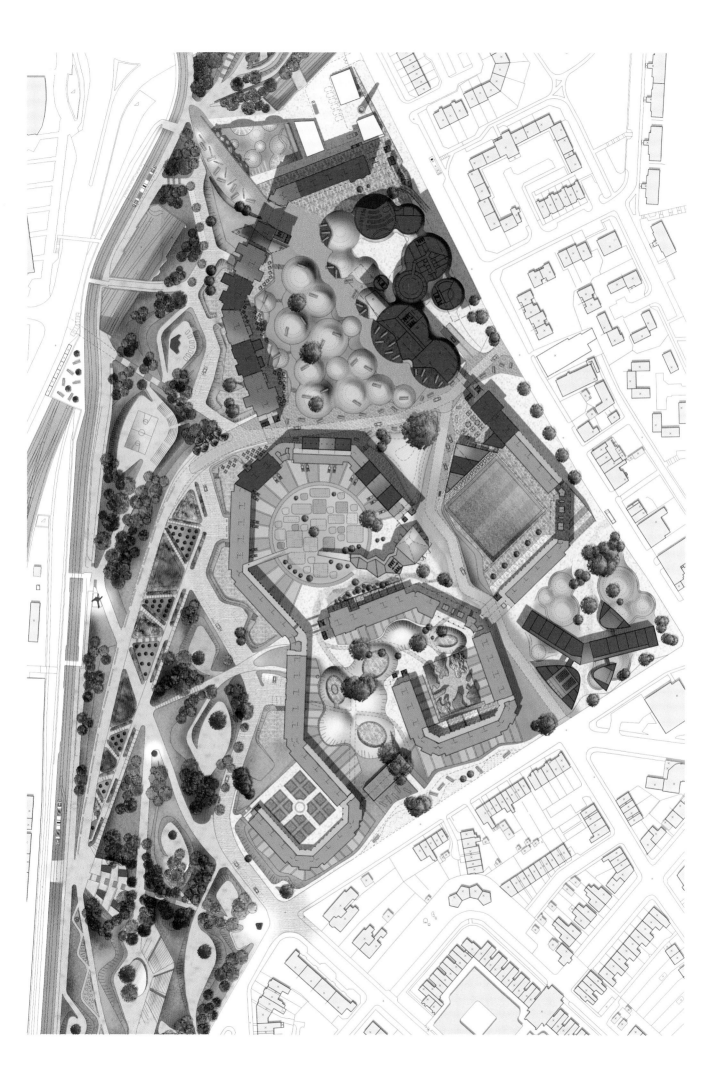

structure. David Bickle is unequivocal: "We felt that this brutal structure needed a level of romance," he says. Hawkins\Brown have introduced a palette of coloured anodised aluminium panels into the elevations and new uses at ground floor to reactivate the public realm. They studied the relationship between landscape and building with Grant Associates. The major change to the estate itself is that it will be set in a new park, linking this new shared public space with a route from Sheffield Station. The lower sections of Parkhill will have smaller private gardens – an anathema to the modernists but necessary if Parkhill is to be a success on the market.

The team of Urban Splash and Hawkins\Brown were then joined by Studio Egret West, who had worked with Urban Splash on the masterplan at New Islington. The creative process of artistic engagement and exchange was fuelled by Jeremy Till's focus on Sheffield in the English Pavilion for the Venice Architecture Biennale in 2006. Hawkins\Brown had just started the detailed planning of the building and new uses with Studio Egret West. They were able to play with their ideas more freely for the exhibition, collaborating with the model-making company Amodels. At the Biennale they were able to present a more abstract proposal that afforded a fresh look at the Parkhill

Above The city-facing façade at night.   Opposite Phase 1 of the scheme
(due for completion in 2011).

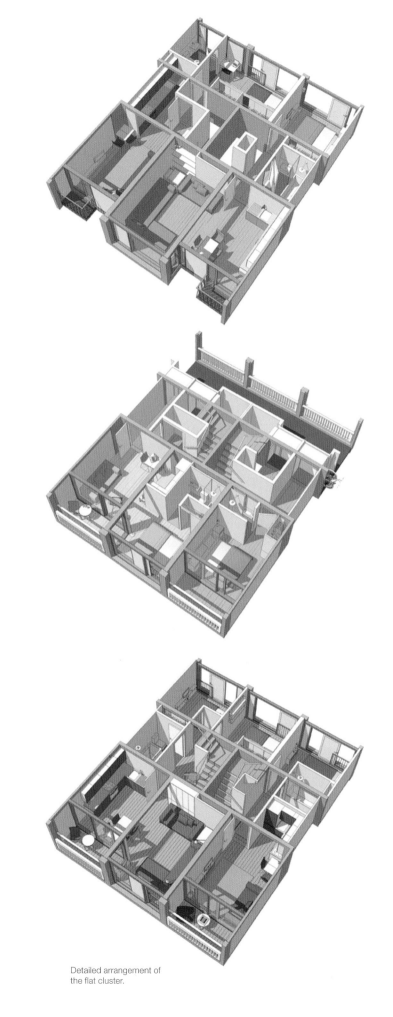

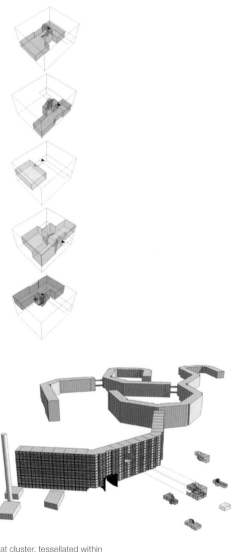

New flat cluster, tessellated within
existing structural grid.

Detailed arrangement of
the flat cluster.

complex. The model romanticised the building by fabricating it from printed silk and jewel-edged Perspex, the forms hovering above the new landscape that had been laser-cut into plates of Sheffield stainless steel. All this was presented under dramatic coloured lighting in the darkened gallery.

To the 'naysayers' at Parkhill, who would either see it torn down or preserved but empty, this romantic approach is a delightful provocation. But back in the real world Hawkins\Brown's determined attitude will prove that modernist post-war housing can be adapted and re-used. For example, one of the architectural criticisms leveled at Parkhill is the way in which the flats offer visual connection out on to the fabled "streets in the sky". Indeed, Ivor Smith described it as one of the most regrettable aspects of his design, and it is something Hawkins\Brown have put right. The streets in the sky will be more passively policed, with windows from hallways and landings keeping an eye on the public realm. It will cater for 21st century lifestyles in the same way that the original proposals responded to mid-20th century living.

Proposed façade treatment to the northeast elevations. The coloured anodised aluminium panels identify the four different streets within the estate which were originally differentiated by brick tone.

Chichester College Redevelopment, West Sussex

Chichester College is a fascinating case study in how to rationalise an educational campus, either rural or urban. Twenty miles from Chichester College's main campus, Brinsbury was still a farm in the 1950s. Today it lies within a 250-hectare estate, still with its own commercial farm. In addition to livestock and arable crops, the estate also has stables for 32 horses. Due to the ad-hoc development that has taken place to convert the farm into a college many of the education buildings are basically sheds without insulation. This was problem enough for an establishment teaching horticulture, but given that Brinsbury is now part of a college, which teaches hair and beauty, engineering, building construction and crafts, drastic improvement was needed to attract students, new business and funding.

Hawkins\Brown's main concept was to provide a welcoming entrance area which would allow the new college to showcase the products of its courses rather than keep them secluded in a 'hotchpotch' of farm buildings. In terms of the rest of the site, Hawkins\Brown introduced a 'village street' as a spine for the developing campus and a single parking area close to the entrance to ensure students and staff could be safely separated from visitors and deliveries. Hawkins\Brown introduced Vogt Landscape Architects to the scheme, they had worked together on Parliament Square. Their landscaping scheme was based on four principles: copses, hedgerows, riparian corridors and garden; the design responded to the local context but within a radical, environmental garden.

In order to reduce the energy costs and make way for new buildings, thirty-two poor quality buildings will be demolished, including glasshouses, workshops and sheds that were being used for teaching. These will be replaced by eight new buildings plus three new buildings on the farm itself. The new structures will be a rethinking of the vernacular of the area, to create a series of single-storey, contemporary barns. A modest palette of three building materials was selected to respond to the local context: glass, timber and metal. The more open buildings, such as the horticulture department, use glasshouses as a model, whilst the Learning Resource Centre is clad in timber to foster and promote a collegiate learning environment.

One can see the same rationalising approach at the main campus, where the focus of the design has addressed a series of 1960s-built finger blocks, which again have been added to over the years in a piecemeal way to no clear plan. The distinctive 1960s gull-wing roofed entrance building, which faces the nearby Chichester Cathedral, will be retained. A single-storey spine that connects four four-storey finger blocks will

Above Hybrid shed\glasshouse concept model for Brinsbury Campus.

Opposite Brinsbury Campus masterplan illustrating arrangement of timber, glass and steel structures.

Above External view of Brinsbury
Campus Welcome Building and
Learning Resource Centre.

Right View of Learning Resource
Centre from 'village street'.

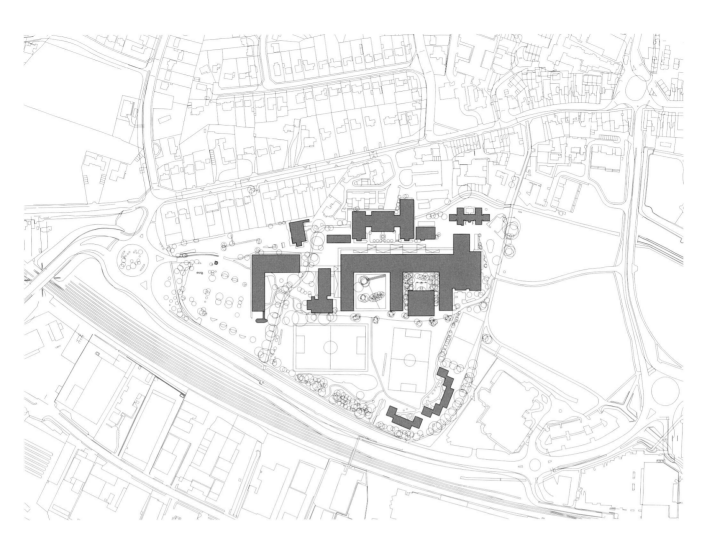

be rebuilt so it matches the height of the older buildings. This will in turn create three distinct courtyards. Working with Vogt, Hawkins\Brown have developed a landscape strategy which provides a distinct identity and purpose for each courtyard and ties the whole project into the wooded belt around the campus.

A new entrance building will be added to the opposite end of the main spine, which faces away from the cathedral towards the main car park and the town beyond. This building will house the more publicly accessible courses, beauty and hairdressing teaching facilities, catering and hospitality suites and a multiple-use performance space. Twelve buildings will be demolished on the Chichester Campus, to rediscover the ordering logic of the central spine and the finger blocks which spur off it.

Both campus masterplans have been developed in close collaboration with Arup structural and environmental engineers. The Brinsbury Campus will use heat generated by an energy centre fuelled by biomass grown locally (either Miscanthus grass or coppiced willow). The Chichester Campus will utilise ground source heat pumps and solar hot water panels. The new buildings on both campuses will be constructed with high levels of insulation and be carefully placed to encourage passive solar heating.

Given the completely different nature of the context and architectural style at Chichester and Brinsbury, it would be understandable if they have been left as distinct projects. Yet Hawkins\Brown felt that some relationship needed to be established – creating a single powerful 'brand'. This link was achieved through the way-finding, graphics and colour schemes developed with long-term collaborators SEA design.

Opposite Chichester College Redevelopment.

Above Chichester College Redevelopment, siteplan (1:5000).

032\
Sevenstone New Retail Quarter, Sheffield

The retail developer Hammerson has become known as a pioneer of town-centre retail across Great Britain and Europe. Perhaps their most famous project is the Selfridges department store in Birmingham, designed by Future Systems. Whatever reservations one might have about the redevelopment of the Bullring Centre, the Selfridges store changed the way that we think about city centres. It is a model that the developer, and particularly its former Development Director Jon Emery, has used elsewhere, most recently with Foreign Office Architects' (FOA) John Lewis store in Leicester. This new model involves not just the use of a signature piece of architecture but a masterplan into which talented architects at varying stages in their careers can contribute. For Sheffield's new Sevenstone district, eight blocks, masterplanned by the interdisciplinary practice BDP, will be designed by eight different architects, with the anchorstone and central showpiece a John Lewis store by O'Donnell + Toumey.

In the summer of 2007 Hawkins\Brown joined BDP, AHMM, Stiff + Trevillion and Foreign Office Architects to contribute distinct buildings that will come together to create Sevenstone. Emery made a point of employing a newer practice, ACME, although its principal, Friedrich Ludwig, was the project architect for the scheme in Leicester.

The block that Hawkins\Brown designed contained elements which had to be retained, including a residential building to the apex of the site and an Edwardian façade. The masterplan required large retail spaces at upper levels and a bridge link to the adjacent block designed by Foreign Office Architects. Even without the connecting bridge it was important that the two blocks had some form of visual link. The set-piece new building by Hawkins\Brown responds to the diagrid structure of the FOA project through its tiling patterns and the triangular recesses of the mansard roof.

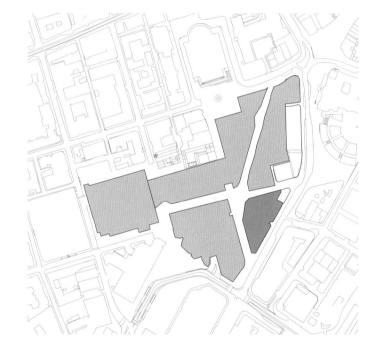

Above Proposed masterplan.

Below Concept model referencing the ornamented surfaces of luxury brands.

Opposite above A raised walkway, lined in gold metal, overlooks the central space, known as Sevenstone.

Opposite below A gilded window at the apex of the building acts as a gateway marker to the new development and frames views of the city.

Next page, left Study model.

Next page, right Elevation, detail referencing Victorian gothic buildings with cast ornament and diaper brickwork in a sensual, dark palette (1:75).

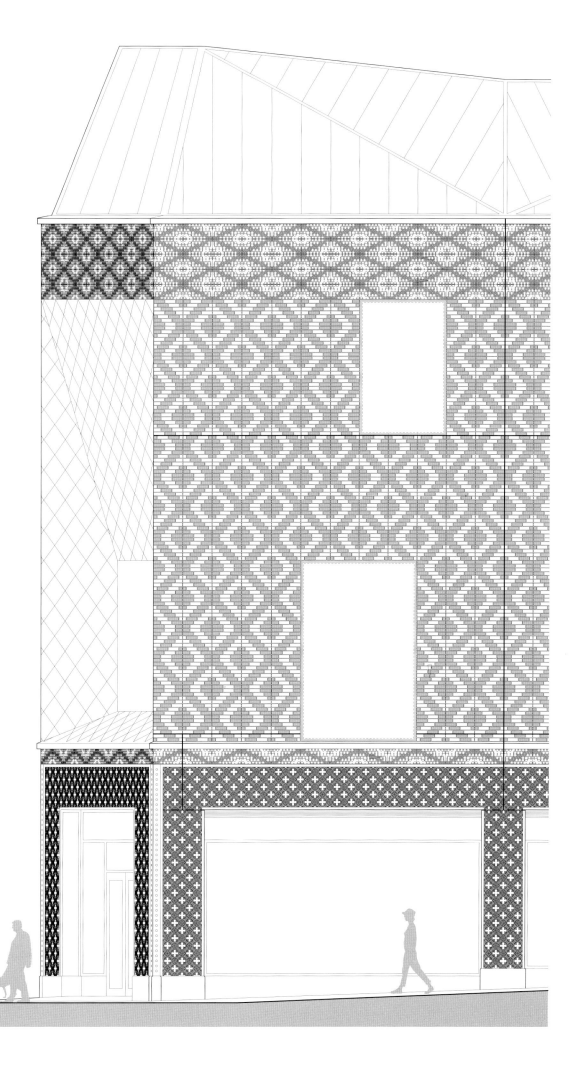

036\

The Wharves, Deptford, London

Deptford is currently the most interesting area for redevelopment in South London. Showpiece projects, like the Laban Dance Centre by Herzog & de Meuron and the Stephen Lawrence Centre, are almost hidden among rusting hulks, old factories packed with new media business and ancient churches. The director of *The Tower* (2007), a BBC documentary about the regeneration of the tower block in the Pepys Estate, caught the significance of the area in a single shot, looking across the water from the mouldering 1960s housing block to Canary Wharf. Deptford is frontier country and so it presents both challenges and opportunities.

In 2007, Hawkins\Brown were asked to assess the development potential for a 4.5-hectare site close to the Thames between Deptford Park and Pepys Park, currently occupied by low-grade industrial warehouses. In the masterplan for the adjacent Convoy's Wharf, Richard Rogers had proposed a diagonal route struck across the Deptford Wharves site. New routes and connections became the generating principles for a new masterplan. The Grand Surrey Canal once ran across the site. The proposal is to reintroduce the water as a new amenity, to attenuate rainwater and to act as a biodiverse, environmental focus for the site.

A crucial planning condition was the local authority's demand that the site be used to attract companies to create 1,200 new jobs. In response a plan was developed for a series of new wharves. Each would have a different character and a mix of uses, determined by the local physical context and the emerging business case. Density and height were varied across the site in response to the neighbouring parks and the new Convoy's Wharf. Hawkins\Brown have created six different types of dwellings: apartments in tower blocks, traditional terraced homes with private gardens, courtyard developments with shared amenities, urban lofts above retail and studio units, high density clusters and individual blocks forming the fourth elevation to Pepys Park.

The practice have considered transport connections across London, investigating alternative approaches such as a riverferry at Greenland Pier, 10 minutes walk from the site; Canary Wharf would be a further five minutes by boat. In a similar way the approach to energy is highly innovative. Hawkins\Brown have worked closely with Max Fordham, sustainability experts, and the client City + Provincial, to harness low-grade waste heat from the nearby South East London Combined Heat and Power energy recovery facility (SELCHP) to provide domestic water heating, space heating and, in the summer, absorption cooling.

Above The scheme is arranged around a re-instated body of water.

Opposite The new wharves are characterised by changes in scale, elevational strategy, brick colour and balcony treatment.

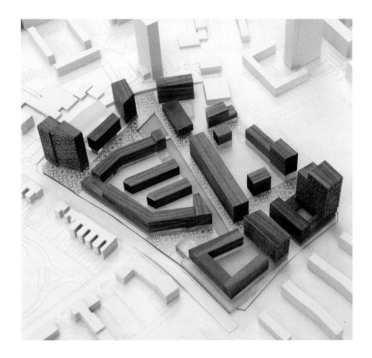

When the Borough of Lewisham was presented with the masterplan, they felt that the brief should be tested with the involvement of other architects and designers. This reflected Hawkins\Brown's own thinking that had questioned whether 4.5 hectares of a city should be authored by one pen. Practices like Gross.Max., Carmody Groake and MaccreanorLavington were invited to help develop the different spirit of each of the wharf areas. This process was overseen by Peter Stewart, a former chair of the Commission for Architecture and the Built Environment (CABE). He has vast experience in assessing the design quality of sites of this scale and acting as a 'critical friend'. It is this process of collaboration that adds to the fine-grained complexity of masterplanning the proposal. A tested vision is one which is more likely to be successful in the long term, and the numerous discussions between architects build a narrative for the scheme. This process has demonstrated how future collaborations at Deptford and other large-scale sites can yield a more creative and fulfilling masterplanning process.

Above and below Detailed view of landscape treatment to public realm.

Opposite Model showing public spaces to early phases.

Highfields Automotive & Engineering Centre, Nottingham

A much overlooked victory for architecture in the last decade has been the manner in which local authorities and private developers have rediscovered their faith in architect-led masterplans, particularly in cases where clients want a more bespoke end product. Nottingham Science Park is a classic case in point. Science parks are often formulaic, and the developers Blueprint, a public-private joint venture between Igloo Regeneration Partnership and English Partnerships and East Midlands Development Agency, asked for a masterplan "which would challenge the traditional approach to the science park". Nottingham Science Park sits on a key site, across the road from the main campus of the University of Nottingham, two miles west of the city centre. The site has long been an eyesore since the first phase of a business park left it a vacant site for medical waste. In the near future Nottingham's new tram system will bring this area back into the town centre.

The design team, which won the competition over 50 other submissions, was composed of Studio Egret West as masterplanners, Hawkins\Brown as architects and Grant Associates as landscape architects. The same team had already worked closely together on the Parkhill redevelopment project in Sheffield.

Although Studio Egret West had more experience as masterplanners, the process of creating the overall concept was shared between the three design studios. The central planning idea consisted of a series of X- and Y-shaped buildings set in a public park with a dramatic pedestrian route over the wetlands connecting the local fishing ponds with the University.

One corner of the site had already been identified by a local further education college as the location for a new automotive and engineering school. This national centre of excellence was planned as a joint venture between Castle College and Toyota GB. It accommodates 350 apprentices from Toyota dealerships around the country, providing opportunities for Nottingham's school leavers looking for a career in the motor industry. Hawkins\Brown were approached by Castle College after they learned about the practice's involvement in the masterplan for the whole site.

Hawkins\Brown designed the new building with Blueprint acting as development managers delivering the project for the College. The Centre was built in 12 months over 2007 – "a big shed of a building" as Russell Brown puts it: 90,000 square feet for just under £10million. Meanwhile Studio Egret West were offered a speculative office building, no. 1 Nottingham Science Park,

Above The buildings are arranged around a central reed bed punctuated by timber lily pad shaped decks.

Opposite Challenging the traditional conventions of science parks, the buildings are dressed in bright green cladding panels.

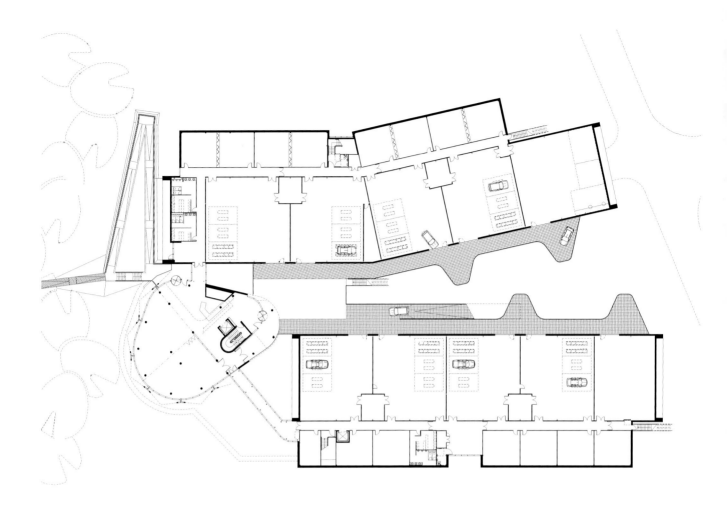

on an adjacent plot. Effectively the practices were making adjustments to the masterplan as they built the two buildings in dialogue with each other. The close cooperation focused in particular on cladding the large industrial buildings in a way that would create a productive response to the almost rural setting.

Hawkins\Brown's final design is still discernible as one of the Y-shaped buildings in the masterplan although the rotunda entrance, known as the Hub, now sits at the front of the building and becomes its public face. Parking is hidden beneath the buildings, behind gabion walls which continue out into the landscape. Elements such as skewed ovoid windows, bullrush motifs and an arhythmic approach to the coloured cladding combine with the giant lilypads to give the first new building in the Science Park a playful 'Alice in Wonderland' feel.

Above First floor plan (1:750).

Below The buildings house facilities for trainee mechanics.

Opposite Bullrush-shaped windows frame unexpected views of the adjacent wing.

Above The Hub is a learning and event space that is wrapped in 'tyre-tread' solar shading.

Opposite Detailed section through the Hub (1:50)

046\
Collaborating
with
Engineers

Good to Talk
by Adam Ritchie

Almost without exception the discussion about collaboration between architect and engineer – what Ove Arup once described as a 'marital' relationship – is centred on the structural engineer. Structural engineering enjoys its revered status because architecture and structure are so closely entwined. Without structure there is no architecture. Prior to the Enlightenment the two professions co-existed with the 'masterbuilder', Brunelleschi, for example, who built the great dome in Florence. Here, then, architect and engineer blurred together. No single event created wholesale fission, but the cracks can be found in France with the introduction of new materials, such as cast-iron and steel, requiring specialist calculation as well as a more 'rational' approach to design. And so, roughly speaking, the gap widened between art and science during the 19th and 20th centuries.

If structure is essential for buildings, it is because of the space it creates and the environment within that space which one experiences directly. One of the most important factors in the design of buildings, and a primary concern of good architecture, is the provision of natural light and its effect on the indoor environment. Thomas Fuller described light as a principal beauty in a building. Similarly, the movement of fresh air to ventilate enclosed spaces has always influenced building form. The visual quality of space has historically been the preserve of the architect, but technological development marked the beginning in a decline of the architect's ability to control the building environment through building material alone. The emergence of this new approach to design brought about a need for an intellectual approach to 'engineering' the indoor environment.

The mechanical engineer's introduction to the process of building design is attributable in part to the intellectual reorganisation of the architectural programme where the functions of building, structural support and building enclosure were first separated by the likes of Le Corbusier, who eschewed the building fabric's role as climate moderator in favour of mechanical systems. His and others' (like Reynar Banham) preoccupation with achieving increasing standards of comfort led to buildings that shunned natural conditions in favour of an artificially created and controlled environment.

The International Style was enabled by the freedom which science and technology now permitted; architecture could be created without climatic influence, "one house for all countries," said Le Corbusier. This liberation fostered a respect for the engineer's role in the design team, leading him to write on the subject: "Our engineers produce architecture, for they employ a mathematical calculation which derives from natural law, and their works give us a feeling of harmony… Now, today, it is the engineer who *knows*, who knows the best way to construct, to heat, to ventilate, to light. Is it not true?" It was true. Many of the greatest buildings of the heroic modernist era are uninhabitable without their mechanical services to cool, heat and ventilate. Collaboration between architect and engineer had become essential.

To understand how these 'marital' relationships became polygamous affairs – modern design teams have myriad of specialist consultants – one must look at the work of Ove Arup, founder of the international consultancy Ove Arup & Partners. Arup's ideal of collaboration required a willingness for the engineer to respect and engage with the architectural language of a design, an ideal developed through collaboration with Berthold Lubetkin during the 1930s. By the early 1960s, Ove Arup & Partners had established the Building Group, later to become known as Arup Associates, which included architects, structural engineers and other designers working together in a joint endeavour. There, a physics graduate called Max Fordham began drawing the mechanical services in complete detail since, typically, the mechanical consulting engineers thought that diagrammatic drawings were adequate to describe their work – an opinion which sadly still pervades parts of the industry today.

The problem was that the amount of building space and design attention given over to concealing the engineering services was growing. Architects were being relegated to becoming decorators of what their 'silo-mentality' engineering consultants designed for them. Louis Kahn succinctly summarised the situation: "I do not like ducts, I do not like pipes. I hate them really thoroughly." In 1966, having understood the need and brief

for a new type of engineer, Fordham left Arup to start a consultancy practice to design engineering services in detail that were made to measure for the buildings they were designed for.

The time was right for a re-evaluation of the relationship between engineering services and architecture. At the same time a Hungarian named Victor Olgyay was developing ideas for his seminal text *Design with Climate: An Approach to Bioclimatic Regionalism* about the intellectual separation between architecture and mechanical services for environmental control; how the building could moderate climatic variations without such significant demands on its environmental systems. The need to conceive of buildings and their systems as a whole would bring benefit both to the integration of the environmental strategies and also lead to reduced energy demand – a relatively alien concept at that time. Environmental Design, as this approach is now known, allied with detailed design integration (for the reduced engineering services that were required) could lead to new and architecturally satisfying solutions.

Architectural integration required an engineer to consider both the mechanical and electrical services in the context of a specific building design, and so design advice could be given under the umbrella of 'building services' represented by one person at design team meetings. In the 1970s, the oil crisis and the perception that fuel was not an infinite resource prompted a shift in direction. At the same time, evidence was mounting that man's reliance on burning fossil fuels could be the cause of major changes to the earth's climate. Both issues fundamentally changed the design agenda for buildings which relied heavily on fossil fuel for heat and power. A new type of consultant was needed who could at once be custodian of the relationship between the environmental function and form of a building's fabric, and master of its technological systems. The environmental engineer was born.

During his time with the Building Group, Max Fordham developed a philosophy that balanced the solution of practical engineering problems with a response to the subjective qualities of a building. Like Arup, Fordham learnt about architecture from working with his architectural contemporaries. Amongst the many lessons Lubetkin taught Arup was that "sensible building must be modified to satisfy the claims of aesthetics". Being prepared to listen and have a broad outlook meant that by the end of an engineer's career many could have made competent architects. Sadly only a few of the schools of architecture or engineering adequately equip their graduates with the skills to work collaboratively with counterparts from other disciplines. For an engineer to work with an architect and vice versa they must at least speak a common language, and while architectural skills may be intuitive, they are skills nonetheless that cannot be learned overnight.

One of the most notable differences in educational styles is the 'crit', an unparalleled ritual in any other discipline. Stopping just short of a public flogging, budding architects must show and explain their work in progress to their tutors, peers and very occasionally a visiting engineer. As an exercise in persuasion of the subjective merits of their ideas these regular crits are good preparation for professional practice where an architect must learn to communicate and justify his or her work to clients, the design team, a contractor or the public at large. Engineers go into professional life without training in the art of persuasion, relying instead on objective laws of physics as proof that their answer is correct and no further persuasion is needed. Architects learn to draw freehand sketches so that their ideas can be communicated on paper in a simple and convincing way. Engineers struggle to compete with this.

A pre-requisite for successful collaboration is that the architect and engineer accept they are different but valued equally for their input to a good building. It is the different levels of ability to communicate that can create tension, especially in modern practice where an increasingly shallow audience can give the means of conveying information as much, if not more credit, than the value of the information itself. No designer can know everything, so they must be able to communicate and share their ideas with others. The most fertile and creative relationships arise between individuals of different backgrounds and views with spheres of overlapping interests.

There has never been such compelling reason for the design community to collaborate as now, with overwhelming evidence that man's activity is irreparably changing the natural environment. Buildings and the energy they consume are only part of the story but an important one nonetheless.

Being considerate of our legacy for future generations has not been a natural consequence of consumerism and the technology-driven, fossil-fuelled revolution in living

Opposite The façade design of the Corby Cube is directly influenced by an early discussion with Adam Ritchie.

standards we have enjoyed. To equate the earth's finite capacity to yield hydrocarbon fuels to a bank account, the most advantaged parts of society have been living off the capital and the interest.

Designers are often pre-occupied by their contribution to society; future generations will hopefully look back at ours and envy the opportunities the situation offered for an intellectual approach to making buildings that are radically better for the people within them and the environment without.

Architects are grappling with the practical and aesthetic consequences of making their buildings more sustainable. The engineering community has been slow in realising the importance of their input to this collective endeavour.

Hawkins\Brown have embraced this new sense of common purpose in a way which does not focus on energy use to the exclusion of other important considerations like cultural and economic sustainability. For over ten years Max Fordham and Hawkins\Brown have collaborated to develop a language of engineering-informed architecture with environmental design inbuilt. This approach respects architecture without the subservience of architectural enabling by engineers, or the converse, that of the rarely beautiful engineering-driven architecture.

Examples in this book include the façade design of the Corby Cube. Despite its geometric form, the distribution of the programme within is spatially planned with the environmental needs – daylight, views and natural ventilation – higher on the agenda than is typical. The auditorium, an environmental 'black box', is placed at the centre of the cube, and the offices, library etc. are flung to the perimeter against the façade. Essentially it is a shallow-plan, high-ceiling, naturally-ventilated building typology around an air-conditioned core. The transparency of the façade modulates according to orientation to limit solar heat gain to the south and allow in north-light, all while keeping a consistent aesthetic, demonstrating subtly the sustainability credentials interleaved in the fabric of the building. Nowhere else in the building is the synthesis of architectural and engineering concern more important than at the façade.

The new Student Enterprise Building for Coventry University shows the same level of co-creativity where an artist, architects, environmentalists, contractors and specialist cladding sub-contractors have designed a striking building skin while incorporating natural ventilation grilles, opening windows, solar control and high levels of insulation.

Architects occasionally fear that engineers are taking over from them, but unless the next generation of engineers is taught to communicate better and think more holistically about the end product, architects will retain their position as the instigator and integrator of sustainable design.

Opposite The glazing palette creates a sophisticated composition that also embraces the environmental requirements of the internal programme.

054\
Corby Cube,
Northamptonshire

Until 2009 Corby was the largest town in Europe not to have a railway station. Now it is only 1 hour 30 minutes away from St Pancras International station in London. In 1950 it was still a small village but was then designated a new town and underwent expansion, with a large number of Scots moving there to work in the steel works. Indeed, the accent in the town is still discernibly Glaswegian. Since 1979, however, when 11,000 jobs were lost at the steel plant, it has suffered from unemployment levels that have, at times, touched 30 percent.

Land Securities, together with Corby Borough Council, are currently working with North Northants Development Company and various government bodies to regenerate the town centre as part of a masterplan for the whole town. The population of Corby is expected to double in the next 30 years through housing on large estates such as Priors Hall, Little Stanion, Oakley Vale and Great Oakley. In anticipation of this, an international, two-stage competition was announced for a new town hall and new arts centre in the town centre.

Hawkins\Brown's winning entry, which proposed placing both programmes in a single building, had such a rigorous logic that it seemed almost inevitable. The civic space of the town hall would be active during the day, and the arts facility would be busy during the evening. Putting the functions of the building together creates economies of scale, but it also results in a livelier building. In the Cube, as the building was nick-named, the library unites the whole building, combining its civic and artistic functions. The library creates an internal street which wraps around the building and is visible on all four elevations. The civic function is stacked on top, and the arts centre is beneath. This makes the library into a thoroughfare, and the chief librarian was only too pleased to have as many people as possible using the facility.

The plan for a fully integrated building was ambitious, and its deep plan makes it difficult to use natural ventilation and daylight in all areas. Although the building appears as a banded glass cube, 50 percent of the external envelope is solid and highly insulated. There are more windows in areas where daylight is needed, such as the library, but in other parts of the striped glass-and-steel façade, such as those facing south, insulated panels are placed behind the glass, resulting in less solar gain. The Cube may look like a glass box, but it functions like a building with traditional windows. As the engineer Adam Ritchie

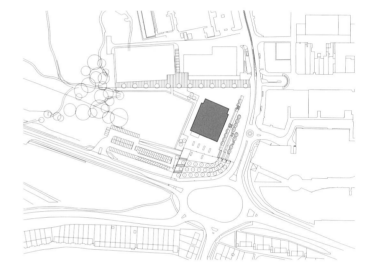

Above Site plan.

Below Unfolded elevation diagram illustrating the modification and articulation of the façade in response to the internal programme and its orientation.

Opposite View of the Cube's entrance from the public square showing the reflective lines of Nayan Kulkarni's proposed 'Blink' installation.

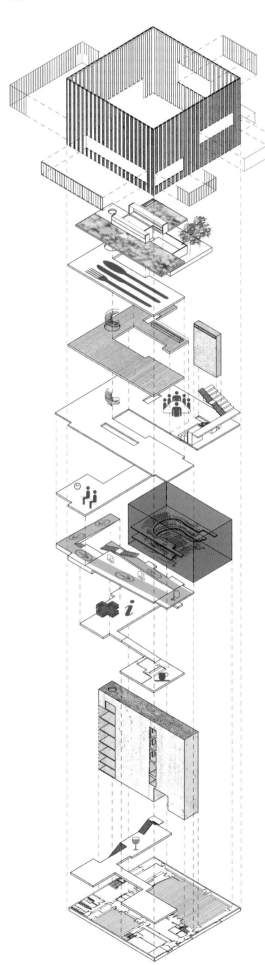

of Max Fordham says in his essay: "Nowhere else in the building is the synthesis of architectural and engineering concerns more important than at the façade." The important collaboration between Hawkins\Brown and Max Fordham has resolved all of these issues to achieve a BREEAM rating of 'Excellent'.

This opacity, achieved through close work with engineers, is carried through the building as a design principle. The council chamber on the first floor overlooks a main street and has a large glazed wall. Corby's citizens can see democracy at work and watch any weddings that may be held there too. The main ambition for the project was to break down the barriers which are traditionally present in a local authority. All of the integrated services are accessible from a single reception area on the ground floor. Visitors can wait in the library for their appointment with the council. The five different organisations who will be based in the Cube are being unified under a single identity which will be carried through into the graphics and the building management.

Apart from its interior functions, the building also had to act as a gateway between the town centre and a more landscaped recreational area and housing development beyond. The architects decided to bring the park to the building: a roof-top garden will be planted with trees, creating an ideal spot for wedding photos and also a setting for civic events. This feature is referred to by the practice as a park, and the impact of Andrew Grant landscaping should not be underestimated. "Too often landscaping is just applied. In this project, landscaping affected the siting of the building from the outset and was treated as an integral part," says Roger Hawkins.

In his capacity as trustee of the Harlow Arts Trust, Roger Hawkins met the wife of the late Sir Frederick Gibberd, the planner of Harlow new town. She recounted how her husband remarked that only in the second part of his career was he able to bring in good engineers. His early career she felt was blighted because he had not worked with good ones at that stage. With an open competition in Corby, Hawkins\Brown were able to bring in the team they wanted, including Grant Associates, Max Fordham and Adams Kara Taylor.

Opposite View of the Corby Cube under construction, showing the cantilevering reading room, July 2009.

Left Exploded axonometric showing the Cube's primary functions within the square plan form and wrapped by the glazed façade.

Above Sectional perspective view of the Cube's interior, showing the theatre to the right, with council chamber and roof terrace above.

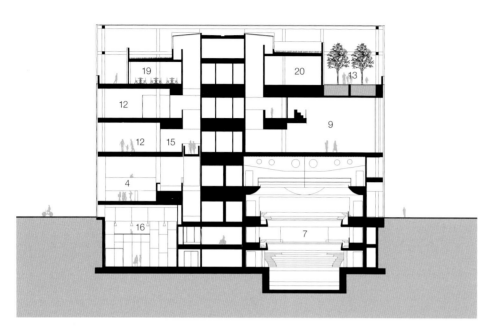

Section (1:500).

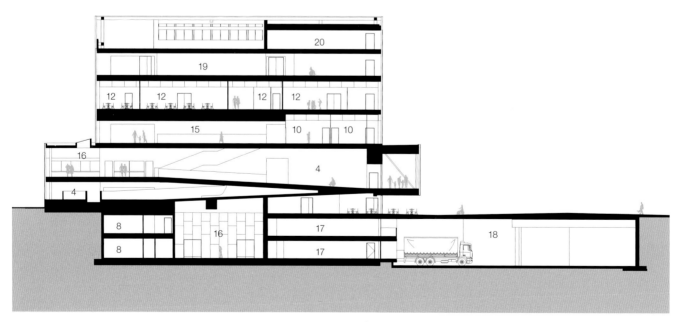

Section (1:500).

1 Reception	6 Kitchen	11 Staff Lounge	16 Studio
2 Foyer	7 Theatre	12 Office	17 Dressing Rooms
3 Box Office	8 WC's	13 Roof Terrace	18 Undercroft
4 Library	9 Council Chamber	14 Store	19 Restaurant
5 Bistro	10 Meeting Rooms	15 Circulation	20 Plant

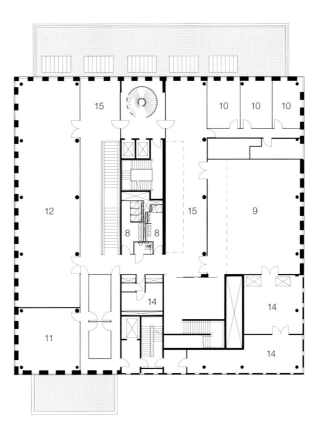

Second floor plan (1:500).

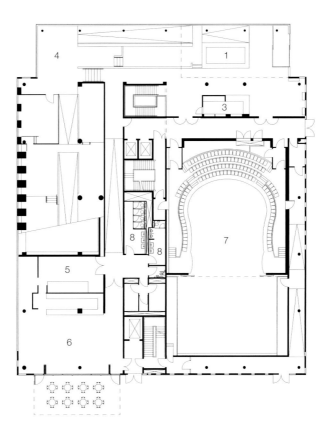

Ground floor plan (1:500).

062\
Stratford Regional Station, London

The sheer complexity of the transport infrastructure required to service the 2012 Olympic Games site finds its knotty apogee in the Stratford Regional Station. By the time of the Olympics the station will provide access to the Central and Jubilee Lines of the London Underground, London Overground, Docklands Light Railway (DLR), the local c2c line to Tilbury and South End as well as National Express East Anglia. This means that half of the station is owned by London Underground and the other half by Network Rail, a circumstance which creates all kinds of challenges when trying to produce a cohesive piece of design.

In addition, the client has changed through the process and is not the owner or an operator. Originally, Transport for London was the client, before it was taken over by the Olympic Development Authority. The importance of the development task cannot be underestimated: around 60 per cent of all spectators visiting the Olympic Park are expected to use Stratford Regional Station, and the legacy will serve the new district created by Stanhope/ Chelsfield to the west of the Olympic Park and the future regeneration of Stratford town centre itself. Further complexity is added by the layers of project management, subconsultancy and technical consultation.

Although there is improvement work to be done across the whole station, the most visible change will be a new mezzanine level providing direct access to the new Central Line and DLR platforms and a new ticket hall that will link with the pedestrian bridge to the Olympic site. The ticket hall echoes the curved roof of Wilkinson Eyre's original station building for the Jubilee Line, which was completed at the end of the last decade. The scheme was given consent following discussions with Chris Wilkinson, who was confident that his building would be sensitively re-developed by Hawkins\Brown. Today, the new ticket hall addresses the familiar profile of the existing building without overly aping its forms.

The bulk of the project is an extensive exercise in architectural 'tidying up'. Hawkins\Brown have introduced eight new lifts and eight new staircases and re-opened disused pedestrian tunnels, all of which will provide better access throughout the station and reduce congestion. They have designed new platforms for the Central Line and DLR, extended two others, consolidated the accommodation for various train operating companies, and removed platform clutter, adding new canopies in its place.

All the materials used in this project had to comply with strict engineering criteria, so the scope for innovation was very

Above A new entrance structure, subways and covered platforms will upgrade and increase the capacity of the existing station in time for the 2012 Olympic Games.

Opposite Early proposals featured sedum planting to the station canopy, creating a large-scale floral pattern visible from the new pedestrian bridge.

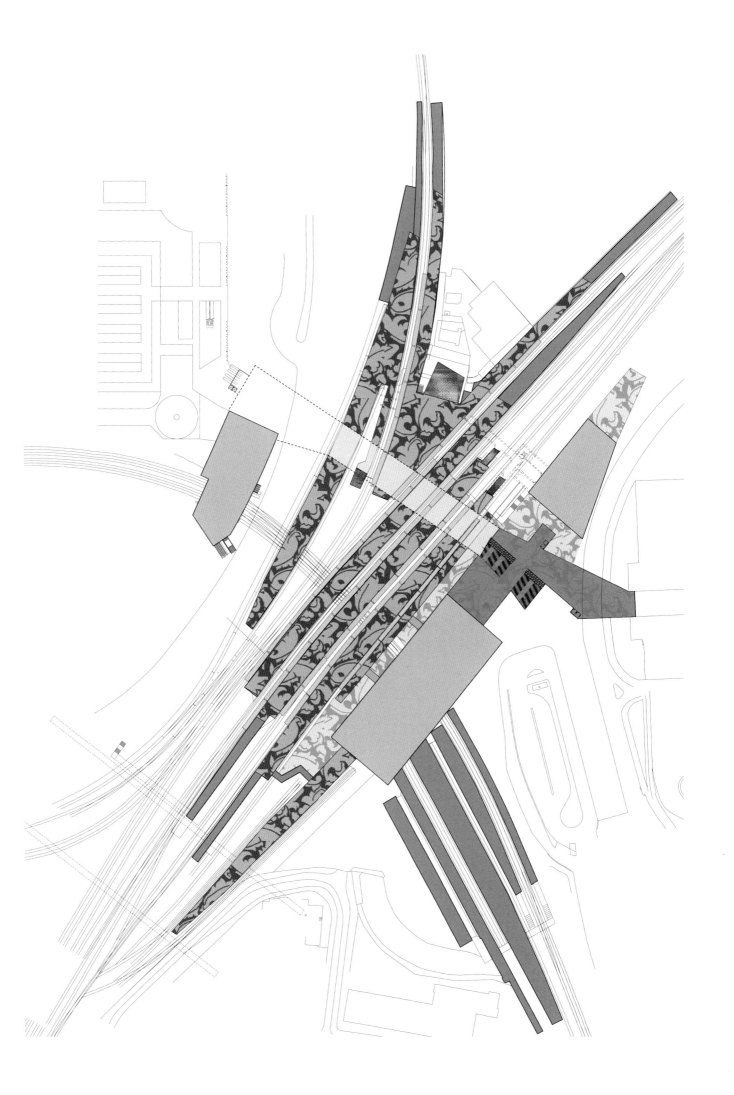

limited. Everything has to be fireproof and, since the fire in King's Cross station in 1987, no timber is permitted. According to legislation introduced in the wake of recent terrorist attacks, all new glazing has to be made from laminated glass. The station's orientation was decided by rail engineers rather than the needs of passengers; Stratford is on a slight incline and, therefore, vertical as well as horizontal sight lines for drivers were critical.

All of this upgrading and rationalisation has to be completed while the station stays open. Stratford is already used by around 37,000 people during the morning peak time. This will rise to 120,000 during the Olympic Games. It is estimated that by 2016 around 83,000 people will be using the station in the morning peak period. The only way to achieve any measure of coherence in this difficult environment has been to constantly champion the design not just with the engineers but with a fluid client body and owners with diverse priorities.

Above When complete, the proposed works will form the gateway for the majority of people travelling to the Olympic site and surrounding new developments. They will form a lasting legacy for East London's imminent transformation.

Opposite left Existing subways have been re-imagined with brightly coloured mosaic tiles.

Opposite right The new entrance connects the existing train station to the Olympic bridge.

066\
Dubai Arts Pavilion, Al Khor Park, Dubai, UAE

Dubai is masterplanned as a themed series of cities. The premise being that when the oil runs out, Dubai will have created a huge amount of cultural capital and will become a tourist attraction in its own right. Even in Dubai, this does not happen overnight.

In an invited competition, Hawkins\Brown were asked to design an arts pavilion that will act as a stepping stone towards a future 'arts city'.

The new building will be sited on the banks of the creek in Al Kohr Park, next to a performing arts centre designed by Rem Koolhaas. He had developed a scheme around an existing outdoor auditorium with a minimal canopy and enclosure. Hawkins\Brown's brief was to create a large amount of gallery space and a destination for touring world-class exhibitions.

With their first scheme on an altogether different site Hawkins\Brown were trying to find an appropriate language and a way of communicating something about the historical, geographical and cultural forces that have shaped this extraordinary place. Taking their cue from Middle Eastern textiles and carpet design, they planned out a complex of buildings within a walled compound, creating an oasis or a mediated environment within the harsh desert of Dubai. The encircling walls and the buildings were pierced with openings reflecting traditional patterns and creating a variety of spaces for display and curation.

However, the client felt that referencing an Arabic vernacular did not sufficiently capture the spirit of this fast-changing society. He wanted to see a design that was developed to the status of an iconic or singular building experience. Indeed, today's Dubai is predicated on this, where the signature moment is an important part of the architectural vocabulary. The second scheme was placed on a different site, creating a sculptural object which cantilevered out over a creek, reflecting and engaging with the water, a particularly valuable commodity in this arid environment.

To keep the structural and environmental impact as low as possible, Hawkins\Brown consulted Arup engineers, who have a great deal of experience in working with different cultures around the world and interpreting client requirements. The same team had worked on Koolhaas's Casa Da Musica in Porto and Hawkins\Brown's Massar scheme in Damascus. In Dubai, given the client's urgent building needs, environmental considerations were of secondary importance, and the collaboration between architects and engineers focused on how such a complex building could be delivered in a twelve-month time frame.

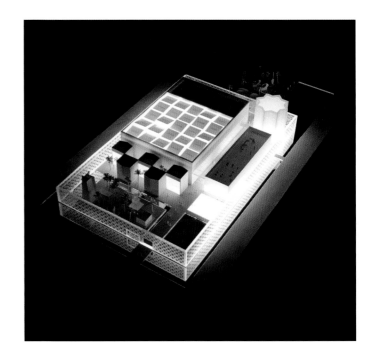

Above The original proposal had a subtle arrangement of gallery spaces and intimate enclosures.

Opposite Site location plan (1:5000) showing the final proposal within the new Al Khor Park on the edge of Dubai Creek.

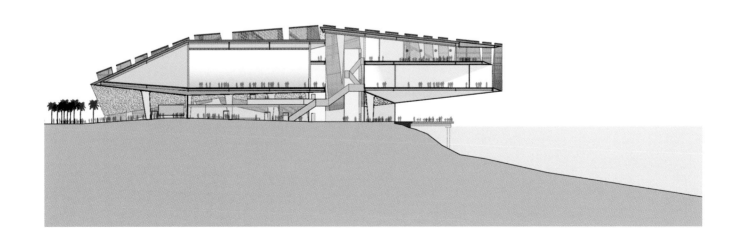

Opposite above The final proposal consisted of an arrangement of galleries and social spaces cantilevering out over the creek, wrapped in aluminium strips.

Opposite below Section (1:500).

Above The grand pavilion entrance provides generous social and amenity space to shelter from the hot desert sun.

Massar Children's Discovery Centre, Damascus, Syria

Massar is a unique organisation set up in 2007 to focus on disadvantaged and excluded children in Syria. Although this non-governmental organisation deals with people at the margins of Syrian society, as a body it has vital political backing. It is an integral part of the Syria Trust for Development, set up by Her Excellency Mrs. Asma Al Assad, the First Lady of Syria. So although Massar began as an itinerant organisation that travelled throughout Syria, performing stories of good citizenship to children, it aims to establish high-profile, well-funded 'discovery centres' in the major cities.

When the organisation set up an international competition for the first centre on a 120,000 square metre site on an old fair ground in Damascus, Massar was still open to ideas about what facilities they should provide and how the ambitions of the organisation could be expressed through a built image. The loose brief for the project was to create a variety of spaces including a museum, a gallery and a school, but they wanted to see what architects could bring to the project development.

The site, although huge, is relatively flat and featureless. It is essentially a gap in the fabric of a crowded city, overlooked by the University and tall international hotel towers. Hawkins\ Brown's scheme looked to create a series of buildings that could be approached by children, where they stepped down into spaces and could climb on the roofs. It was deliberately anti-institutional and non-monumental, more an inhabited landscape than a single building. The landscaping and architecture would fold and wrap around the site. The metaphor of a 'carpet' provided a sense of one continuous fabric, with the landscape becoming the building, and the building becoming the landscape, but also built on local cultural references and the way Massar operated through storytelling in villages.

The competition team included Mark Harrison to help with briefing in collaboration with school children, Grant Associates and Arup Engineers. Together they presented themselves as a group who could use their existing working relationships to create an environmentally responsible building. Work on natural ventilation provided a model for the sections of the buildings. Wind scoops would bring fresh air into the low-lying, semi-submerged buildings, which are formed by excavation and shotcrete sprayed onto mesh. The buildings represent naturally cooled, concrete tents or perhaps grottos, integrated with the Syrian landscape and the local micro-climate.

Above Sketch section showing the variety of activities taking place in a continuous undulating landscape.

Below Concept model showing the textured pattern of facilities forming a 'carpet'.

Opposite A concentration of children's learning facilities bulge from the landscape, forming a focus for the project.

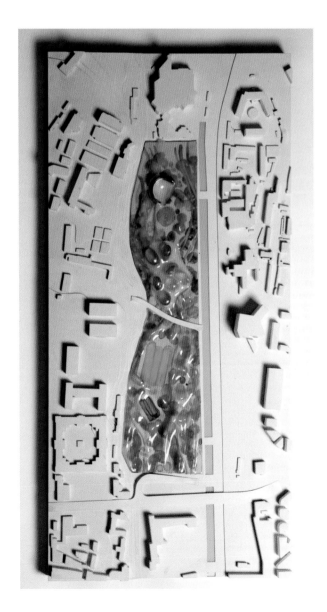

Tottenham Court Road, Crossrail Station, London

In an article in the *London Review of Books* in 2000, the architecture critic Andrew Saint explained how the architect Roland Paoletti was given a free rein on the Jubilee Line Extension in London more by luck than by judgment. Saint believed that this singular piece of public spending oversight had led to great architecture. "There can have been few occasions when London has seen so many aspiring works of architecture on the same theme opened simultaneously; a parallel with the City churches built after the Great Fire is not out of place," he wrote.

Crossrail, the major new railway connection from Maidenhead and Heathrow in the west, through 21 kilometres of new tunnels under central London to Shenfield and Abbey Wood in the east, will be different. The project is engineering-led, resulting in a different role for the architect. Rather than separate commissions, Crossrail have created a delivery system combining all disciplines, allowing design to flourish within engineering constraints. Hawkins\Brown's part of the Arup Atkins Hawkins Brown (AAHB) team which has been co-located at a separate office in Canary Wharf, creating a team of around 60, including 10 architects. Working from the same computer model in the same office, the architects will help form the shape and feel of the Dean Street ticket hall, providing new links to Soho.

Hawkins\Brown are already working with London Underground and Halcrow on the existing Tottenham Court Road station in front of Centre Point and the corner of Oxford Street, ensuring that the most prominent parts of the two projects have a continuous architectural concept. A total of £1 billion investment is being made, bringing an additional 1.5 million people within 60 minutes of London's key business districts. Sitting right in the heart of the City it is a massive and hugely important piece of infrastructure. In addition, the architecture has to integrate an over-site development, which is expected to be redeveloped two or three times during the projected lifespan of the new station. The lid of the station box is 8 metres above ground level, forming a base for a new residential development also being designed by Hawkins\Brown.

Safety is a fundamental consideration for the scheme, and the provision for smoke extraction in the case of an emergency is of huge size. The architects are working around three large fans, the equivalent of jet engines, which must be housed above ground and be accessible by maintenance staff. In addition there need to be means of escape – staircases that can be

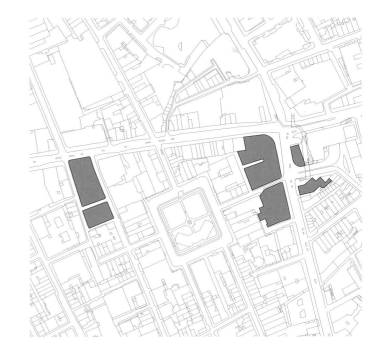

Site plan showing the existing Tottenham Court Road Station to the east and the proposed new Crossrail station to the west in Soho.

pressurised to prevent smoke access in the case of fire – and a means of entry for emergency services.

At basement level, from which point users can descend by another escalator either to the Central Line or to the Crossrail, an intermediate concourse is required. At this juncture, Hawkins\ Brown have suggested introducing natural light from above: it is the simplest form of way-finding in a subterranean environment.

The Crossrail platforms are 200 metres in length and to help orientate emerging passengers the character of each end of the station is subtlety adjusted using artwork and lighting to reflect the differences between the bright new piazza outside Centre Point and the narrow intimate streets of Soho.

Above Sectional perspective of the western ticket hall and lower concourse.

Below The western entrance will feature an integrated digital art wall.

Next page The complexity and scale of the project is revealed by the plan (1:1000).

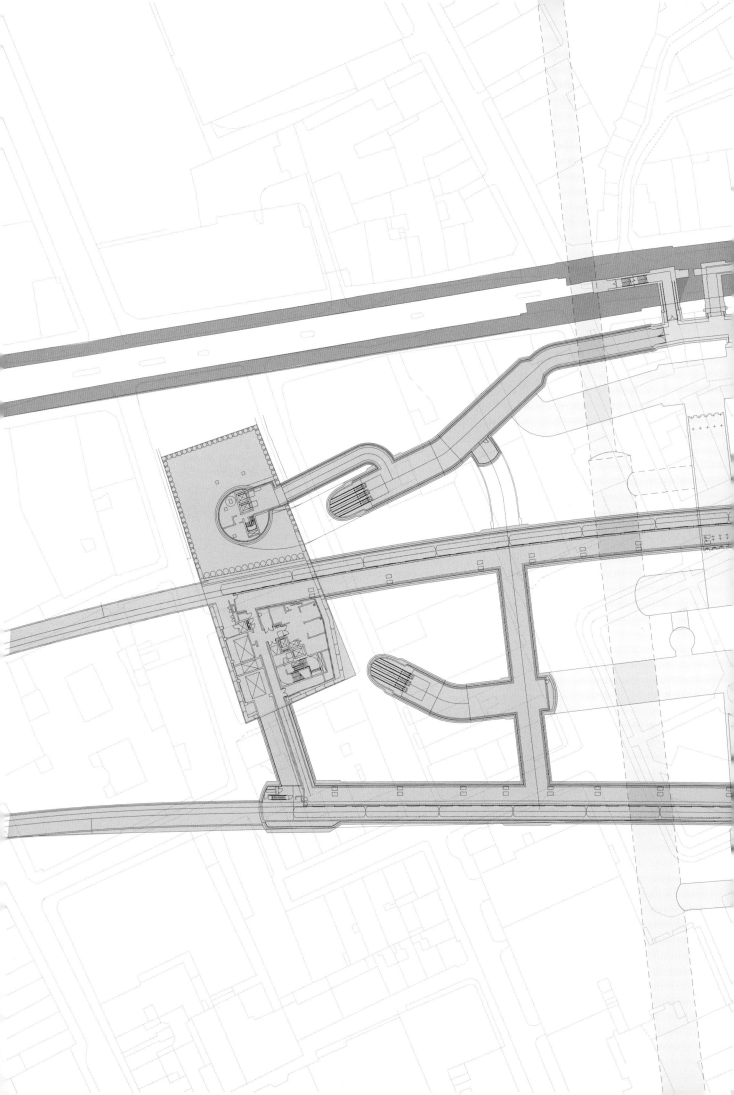

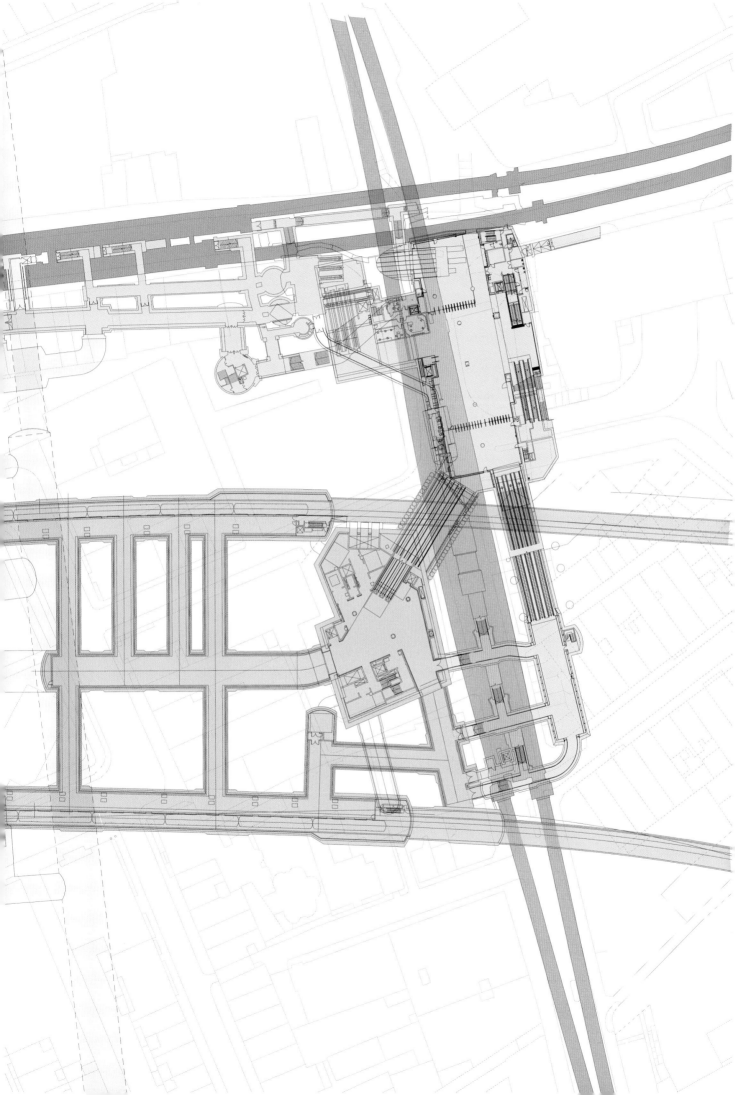

Dublin Metro North, Dublin, Ireland

One of the fundamental contradictions of transport planning, particularly for rail, is that the place where the traveling public needs a station is often the most difficult place for the engineers to meet the technical constraints of the rail system. While the engineers are focusing on track alignment, site access and avoiding services to other buildings, the architects are seeking out the busiest sites in the city. The necessary compromises and negotiations are an important lesson for architects working in an engineering-led team.

Dublin Metro is effectively a subterranean tram system which will connect the city to its airport, from St. Stephen's Green all the way to Lissenhall through Seatown and Nevinstown. This in turn will create a spine for new development to the north of the Irish capital. Hawkins\Brown were introduced to the project by Jacobs Engineers, who had in turn been civil engineering consultants for the architects on the early stages of Tottenham Court Road, and who were working with Hawkins\Brown on Stratford Regional Station in East London. In Dublin, Jacobs and Hawkins\Brown's role was to establish the design parameters at an early stage of the project, providing feasibility studies and defining the requirements of the client, the Rail Procurement Agency (RPA).

The route of the new railway had largely been defined, but it was important for future development to know the best sites for stations in a general location. In order to familiarise himself with the area, Roger Hawkins walked the route out to the airport and collaborated with a local practice, McCulloch Malvin. Effectively, Hawkins\Brown became the interface between the local architects and the engineers, and the lead designers for presentation to the local authorities.

Over a year's work in 2006, Hawkins\Brown developed a series of long, linear stations that were cut into existing streets without the need for large-scale demolition. Specific recommendations were made for areas such as Ballymun, where the tramline would run above ground through the town's main street.

Throughout the process Hawkins\Brown worked closely with the engineers to understand and balance the practicalities of delivering a new railway with the regeneration potential of new stations and a respect for the historic fabric of Dublin.

Diagram showing the engineering strategy that will be adopted between the proposed stations along the new line.

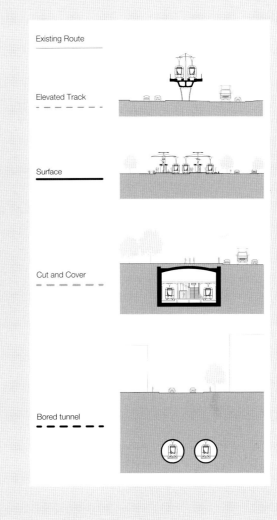

Existing Route

Elevated Track

Surface

Cut and Cover

Bored tunnel

078\
School of Arts, University of Kent, Canterbury

If a back lot is used as a set in a film, it is done to confuse the audience. This can be either for comic effect, as in the last sprawling fight in Mel Brooks' *Blazing Saddles*, or for an alienating affect, as in David Lynch's *Inland Empire*. Film lots are anti-architecture. They are a series of sheds which are closed, blank and erected without care, so that imaginary worlds can be created within them. The buildings are close to each other to allow people to get to their chosen set as quickly as possible. Hawkins\Brown have used this entirely un-civic model as the cue for their design for a new School of Arts at the University of Kent in Canterbury.

For this invited competition, the practice was expected to create a building that would bring the drama, film and visual arts departments, currently spread across the campus, into one building. The site provided is effectively the gateway to the whole campus, sitting on a central roundabout but enclosed by unremarkable buildings on all the other sides.

Working closely with the acoustic engineers, the practice decided to separate the film and sound studios physically from the rest of the building fabric to provide necessary acoustic isolation and then to put them in a larger box to create the circulation space. The black box drama studios are pushed to the northern edge of the building, away from the traffic noise and sunlight. The space between the boxes became important for break-out spaces, i.e. an area for various kinds of programmed and chance encounters and interdisciplinary work.

As well as creating programmatic divisions, these boxes also act as sculptural forms behind the double-height glazed façade. The glass has an embedded mesh to help control heat gain in the day, but when lit from inside it becomes quite transparent. This means that the first, timber-clad box can be distinguished from the one decorated with an Op Art pattern and from the third, which has a more conventionally striped exterior. Small bridges provide links between the blocks, and on the second floor there is a ring of academic offices, which were originally imagined as a series of beach huts. While this ambition was scaled down in favour of more familiar academic offices, they have retained the charm and random sequence of colours from the original concept.

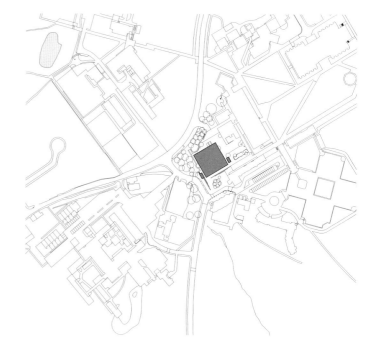

Above Site plan (1:5000).
Opposite above The building is conceived as a series of loose 'boxes' housing the drama, film and visual arts facilities.

Opposite below At night the lower floors reveal the less formally articulated circulation and breakout spaces between the boxes.

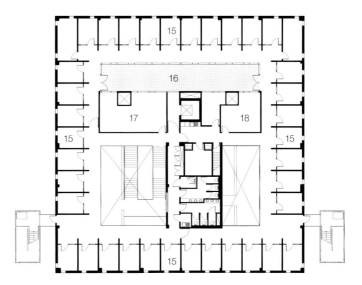

Second floor plan (1:500).

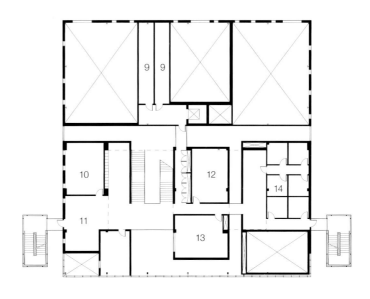

First floor plan (1:500).

Ground floor plan (1:500).

Opposite above A variety of informal learning spaces encouraging collaboration and chance encounters.

Opposite below The boxes are differentiated by material but retain a strict monochrome palette. Splashes of red identify key elements.

1 Drama Studio
2 Practice & Research Studio
3 Art & Design Studio
4 Social Space
5 Recording Film Studios
6 Entrance Lobby
7 Technicians Office

8 Store
9 Control Room
10 Digital Studio
11 Post Graduate Study Area
12 Film Production Teaching
13 Specialist Teaching
14 Edit Suites

15 Academics Office
16 Roof Terrace
17 Administrators Office
18 Part-Time Teachers Office

Taipei Performing Arts Centre, Taipei, Taiwan

The Taipei Opera House is quite literally more than just a building. It is an intervention that will work on the level of a masterplan. The stipulation in the competition brief for three performance spaces, an opera theatre, a studio space and a medium-sized repertory venue, encouraged the design team to create three linked structures that will create a new arts quarter in Taipei and transform this part of the city. Another key element of the brief, and a particularly inspired one, was the acknowledgement of the proximity of the famous Shilin market, which comes alive at night with alleys of food vendors and becomes crowded by gastronomes in search of oyster omelettes and tempura. According to Seth Rutt, "we found that there was a lot of permeability in the existing urban grain. So, in our proposal, the theatre spaces formed the building core and the spaces between them became public." In the competition scheme, the building's volumes are cut back to create dramatic views of Shilin.

Researching East Asian drama in preparation of the design, the architects found references to the idea of a trinity: tea-picking operas, created by the Hakka people who immigrated from China, feature three fixed characters covered in richly ornamented costumes or veils. Inspirations such as this led to the creation of three separate volumes that are linked by a spiraling walkway and then thinly covered in a glass veil that rises at certain key points to create entrances. Considered as part of Hawkins\\Brown's output, the Taipei Opera House is very much a sister building to the Corby Cube. The creation of an undercroft for services permits the whole ground floor to be a public space, and the ingenious entrance system permits large, complex sets to be delivered without hindering the public use of the building.

The Taipei Opera House project shows how architects need engineers. Its intricate and highly specific design is only made possible by the close working relationships, not only with Arup engineers, but also with specialist theatre architects, in this case Iain Mackintosh of Theatre Projects. Again, the landscape architects Grant Associates were important contributors to the overall design, proposing a roof garden planted with blossom trees. Open, green space is very limited in Taipei so the scheme makes a very public gesture of offering a place to have lunch or perform early morning Tai Chi. Indeed this element is not just an afterthought or add-on but an expression of the building's openness.

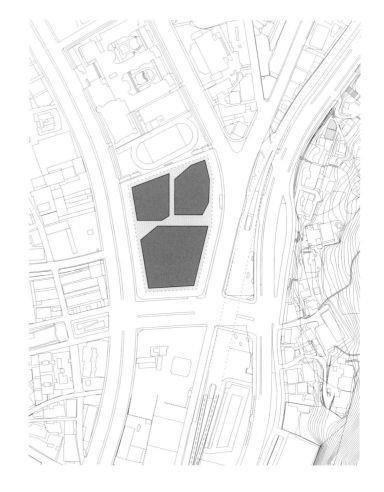

Above The three theatres are grouped as an ensemble around the main foyer like the characters from a Hakka Tea Opera.

Opposite The veiled façade references the Taiwanese symbol of the five-petalled plum blossom.

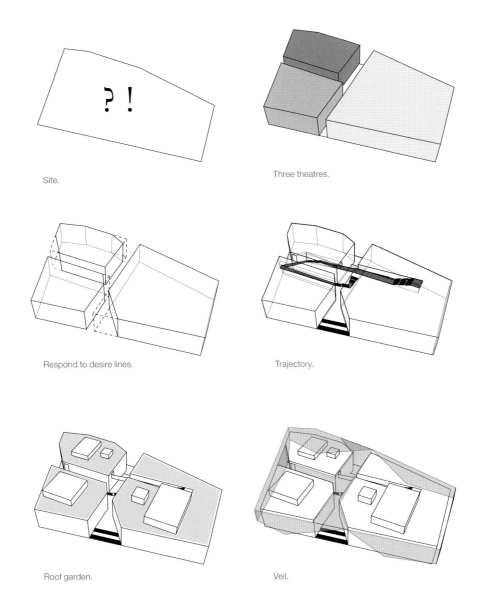

Site.

Three theatres.

Respond to desire lines.

Trajectory.

Roof garden.

Veil.

South elevation.

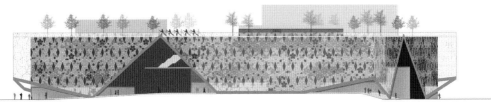

North elevation.

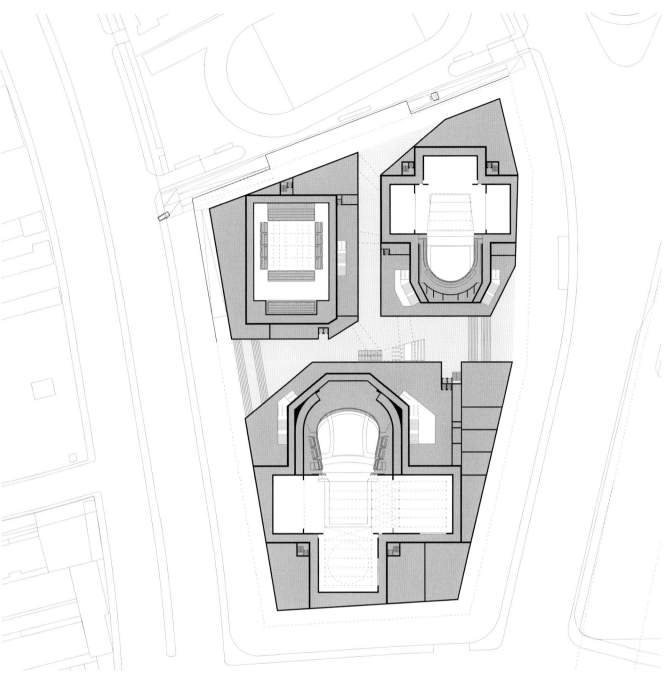

Ground floor plan.

West elevation.

East elevation.

088\
Collaborating
with
Artists

Architecture on a Plinth
by Jes Fernie

It took thirty years for the architectural avant-garde to recover from Adolf Loos' statement that "the omission of ornament is a sign of intellectual strength". It was not until 1943 that Sigfried Giedion challenged the modernist orthodoxy on ornamentation. Working under the auspices of CIAM (Congrès International d'Architecture Moderne), he argued that modern architecture in undecorated form was mute and that it needed art to give it some form of symbolic meaning. It was not until the much-maligned years of postmodernism in the 1970s and 80s – certainly maligned in contemporary architecture criticism – that the first real opportunities arose for artists to effect the built environment. It was at this point that we saw the beginnings of the numerous collaborations between artists and architects that we take for granted today.

The explosive growth of collaborative practice between artists and architects that followed postmodernism can be crudely divided into three decades which takes us from 'clunky' 1980s add-ons, to 1990s dictatorship to the eclecticism in the 2000s. In the 1980s, the 'Percent for Art' drive from local authorities established a space in which artists could form a dialogue, however superficial, with architects to create works that were at best worthy and at worst tokenistic. Artists such as Claes Oldenburg and William Pye were heralded as the high priests of bravado in the public realm. Lonely spaces in corporate landscapes were filled with empty statements in the form of monumental sculptures. This kind of art was not pretty but it did establish the groundwork for the more interesting relationships to come.

The 1990s saw a more mature dialogue. Practitioners, clients and funders began to recognise the value of introducing an artist's voice into a design team even if their contribution did not necessarily end in a physical form. The most astute practitioners learned that questions are often more powerful than statements – whether these statements are sculptural or verbal – and artists became increasingly called upon to challenge assumptions about, and approaches to, architectural projects. This enthused architects eager to claw back some of the thinking time that the rise of planning authorities and project managers was increasingly stripping away.

Tania Kovats' work with Axel Burrough of Levitt Bernstein Associates on the Ikon Gallery in Birmingham in the mid-1990s is often quoted as an early example of an artist working with an architect on a conceptual level. Kovats asked the design team (and herself) to consider what would happen if they put the gallery itself on a plinth? What would it mean metaphorically and practically? It was a deeply provocative statement that managed to encompass the monumental and the invisible in one fell swoop. Architect Levitt Bernstein acknowledged that Kovats was an important member of the design team and conceived the dark slate plinth upon which the converted school building now rests.

At the same time Hawkins\Brown were working with Nicky Hirst at the University of Birmingham, and with Richard Wilson, Peter Doig and Martin Richman at the University of Portsmouth Student Centre.

In some quarters the mantra of artists' inclusion in design teams, particularly in the case of buildings for the purpose of exhibiting art, became overly dictatorial. It seemed for a while that all architects were forced into accepting that if they did not work with an artist, their scheme would be lacking an artistic sensibility or integrity. An absurd idea that Rem Koolhaas, who has become known for his conversations with artists, has often commented on, extending his dislike of the dictat to his refusal to believe that every time an artist and architect come together something great happens. Indeed, in contemporary society the long-held belief in the redemptive power of art has made something of a resurgence. Often an architect will announce that they are collaborating with an artist as if this is somehow morally improving. Let us not forget that when an artist and architect come together sometimes something awful happens.

Hawkins\Brown were well aware of the fact that there were only a small number of very particular projects which presented an opportunity for them to form a close dialogue with an artist. It is rare indeed for it to be appropriate for an artist to be involved, rarer still that the client will be committed and funding will available. Having established the practice in the late

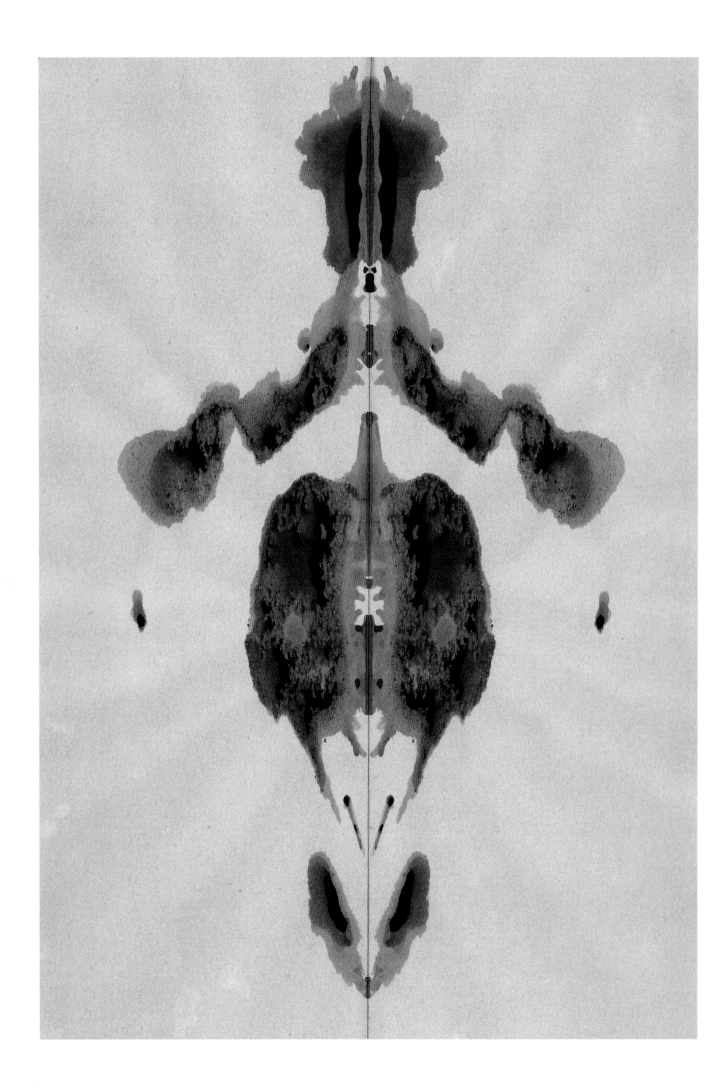

1980s, they were becoming significant players in the British architectural landscape by the early 1990s, and they began to develop their long-standing interest in art by channeling their conversations with artists into their working process. In 2001 director David Bickle invited photographer and filmmaker Andrew Cross to consider how a small public square in Dalston, East London, might be rethought and repositioned for a broader, more inclusive audience.

Cross made a photographic study of the area and, along with Bickle, devised a hair-brained scheme to create an opportunity for members of the public to view the building site from a crane, creating a democratic vantage point, usually only accorded to the design team members and the client. A little later, in the mid-1990s Bickle was taken with Kovats' Ikon intervention in Birmingham and has often cited this project as a major influence on his thinking about the possibilities for artists' engagement with the process of architecture.

At the same time, students in art and architecture schools were taking their cursory nods at one another a step further by developing long-standing collaborative relationships. Artists became interested in working on a much larger scale. Indeed, in an art world determined by decisive turns in art practice since the late 1960s, by the 1990s artists were expected to work on a large scale. Many artists were still toying with the idea of a social sculpture in which art would transform society, as proposed by Joseph Beuys. Land Art filtered through the practice of Gordon Matta Clark and was making itself felt in art colleges. If art wanted to influence society, one of the best ways it could do so was by addressing that most social of art forms, architecture.

Architects meanwhile were keen to develop conceptual languages of expression through engaging with art practice. With the demise of modernism and its overarching set of functional principles, architects not taken by the easy fix of postmodernism, looked to new areas for a conceptual framework. The art world with its more dynamic intellectual atmosphere was ripe for plundering. David Adjaye and Chris Ofili met at the Royal College of Art in London in the early 1990s, when Adjaye was studying architecture and Ofili painting. They have worked together ever since, Ofili contributing ideas for patterns on the surfaces of Adjaye's buildings and Adjaye contributing ideas for gallery installations in which Ofili's paintings can be set.

It is Herzog & de Meuron however who have shown how collaboration with artists on a conceptual level can invigorate architecture in a more exciting fashion. Their interest in forming dialogues with artists such as Thomas Ruff and Remy Zaugg lent a powerful currency to their proposals and formed a major part of their rise to architectural stardom. Their collaboration with Michael Craig-Martin on Tate Modern and the Laban Dance Centre, established their British credentials, but it was their work with Ai Wei Wei on the Beijing National Stadium in 2008 which presented an international face to the scope of possibilities that collaboration with an artist could offer. There is no overt separation between art and architecture in the project, no object in a plaza, but instead a seamless amalgamation of art and architecture that has evolved out of a series of conversations about the social and cultural context in which physical statements are made.

This loosening up of the rules has been a defining feature of the last decade; a diverse, eclectic area of practice between artists and architects has developed. This is creating a more level playing field between the two disciplines. Instead of working within the limits set by architects and clients, artists are challenging the architectural world by appropriating the public realm as well as the language of architecture in unprecedented ways. Artists are increasingly bold in their determination to have a dialogue with the city, influencing the mood and atmosphere of the streets. When designing a new square or a park, local authorities are as likely to turn to an artist as an engineer or an architect.

Swiss artist Pipilotti Rist actively looks for opportunities to do projects in the public realm before a competition is devised to invite her proposal: "In these big public schemes, there's this bloody crazy, bad situation that you have to wait to be asked to be involved. I always try to be faster and propose something first." Rist's hugely successful red carpet, designed in collaboration with architect Carlos Martinez for a small town in Switzerland, is a playground for children, adults and cars. It brings a dynamism and sense of life to a previously disused part of the town and shows the huge impact an artist can have on the physical environment, given the opportunity.

When interviewed for their first book, *&\also*, Russell Brown explained what they had appropriated from art practice into their own: "Artists seem to be able to tackle the bigger questions, be they practical, philosophical or just human. They are seeking a much more direct communication with their audience, they are less hidebound by formulae,

Opposite 'Rorschach' inkblot on paper by Nicky Hirst for New Biochemistry building, University of Oxford.

rules and doctrines. They seem to be fearless in their pursuit of a great, populist, funny, extraordinary idea."

Hawkins\Brown brought Nicky Hirst in to work with them on a scheme for the Biochemistry Department at Oxford University (*Glass Menagerie*, 2009). The ink blot drawings on the façade of the building (just one part of a much larger commissioning programme) form an extravagant and intriguing dialogue with the new public square in which it is situated, which comes alive in the evening when the shapes become voids. Hirst worked closely with Morag Morrison and in a telling display of the architects' commitment, formed an intense two-year dialogue. Morrison's in-depth knowledge of contemporary art and the ways in which artists work played a crucial role in the success of this collaboration.

While Morrison was grappling with the glass contractors at Oxford, another architect, Seth Rutt, was introducing the work of Sarah Staton into Hawkins\Brown's work for Hammerson at Sevenstone in Sheffield. He sensed that an artist could take the decorative themes from the victorian buildings that surround the project and find patterns that would blur the boundary between the new and the old.

Over their 21-year life span, Hawkins\Brown have witnessed, and been part of, the rich development of collaborative practice between artists and architects. One of their most recent collaborations has been with Bob and Roberta Smith's *Faîtes L'Art, pas La Guerre* (Make Art, Not War), 2008, shortlisted for the Fourth Plinth commissioning programme in London's Trafalgar Square. Smith's competition proposal for the empty plinth was powered by the sun and designed in collaboration with David Bickle at Hawkins\Brown.

We have reached a moment where the rules have been frayed and the possibilities are open-ended and dynamic, heralding a bright future. The argument for an artists' inclusion in design teams or involvement in the public realm no longer has to be made and that there is now a well-established system to support artists through the process. In fact, artists are playing an increasingly discursive and significant role in the formation of our public spaces and in so doing they are broadening the scope of architectural practice. Even so, David Bickle, Morag Morrison and others at Hawkins\Brown are only too aware that the system relies heavily on the visionary sensibilities of the clients, developers and local authorities who are, largely, in control of the way in which our towns and cities look. The considerable inroad into collaborative practice that has been made over the past thirty years is, to a large part, in their hands.

Opposite The artwork has been translated into the glazing of the finished building.

The New Art Exchange, Nottingham

At the turn of the 21st century a number of high-profile arts buildings were built across Great Britain, using public money from Government and the National Lottery that had been distributed by the Arts Councils of England, Scotland and Wales. While a project such as the Walsall Art Gallery, which was given £21 million of public funding, opened to plaudits and awards for its architecture, conspicuous failures such as the National Museum of Pop in Sheffield established a reputation for Arts Council projects coming in late and over-budget. The New Art Exchange in Nottingham was planned and developed in this climate of self-criticism. As a result, the client and the design team were kept on a very tight budgetary leash for what was a modest building in the first place.

The New Art Exchange was formed in 2003 as a partnership between an arts group focused on South Asian arts and a second group which supported the development of artists of African/Caribbean origin. The two organisations shared offices in an aging dispensary on Gregory Boulevard in the heart of the Hyson Green district of Nottingham, sandwiched between a Victorian library and an Edwardian building now used as a community centre. Hawkins\Brown became closely involved in helping the new organisation through the funding application process with the Arts Council which eventually provided about £2.6 million from the £4 million budget, with matchfunding from Nottingham and East Midlands Regeneration Funds.

The collaboration between the New Art Exchange and Hawkins\Brown benefited from the fact that both Russell Brown and Roger Hawkins are from Nottingham, although their practice is based in London. Their connections enabled the practice to introduce artist Hew Locke, who created a ceiling installation for the new art centre. Locke is represented by Hales Gallery, which is based in the Tea Building in Shoreditch, London's new centre for media and creative industry. The building's interior was designed by Hawkins\Brown, and Hales have worked with the architects on a number of schemes, introducing artists and managing the commissioning process.

Locke is perhaps best known for his collaged sculptures of the British monarchy. The piece that first established him in the British art scene was *Cardboard Palace* (2002), which drew on the language of pavilion architecture. A maze of curved bays and alcoves, the installation was punctured by backlit portraits of Princess Diana and Queen Elizabeth II.

The New Art Exchange had identified the ground floor cafeteria as the site for Locke's work, deciding that it should be obviously distinct from any other artwork in the ground floor gallery. Locke adapted his creative process to reflect the

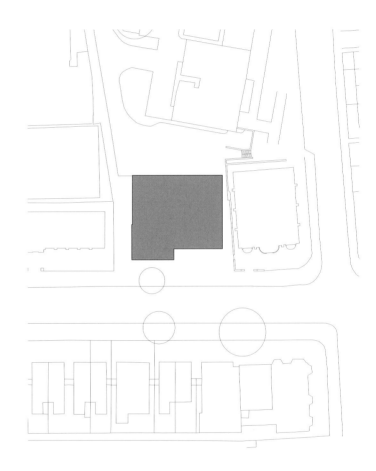

Above **Site plan** (1:1000).   Opposite **South elevation** (1:200).

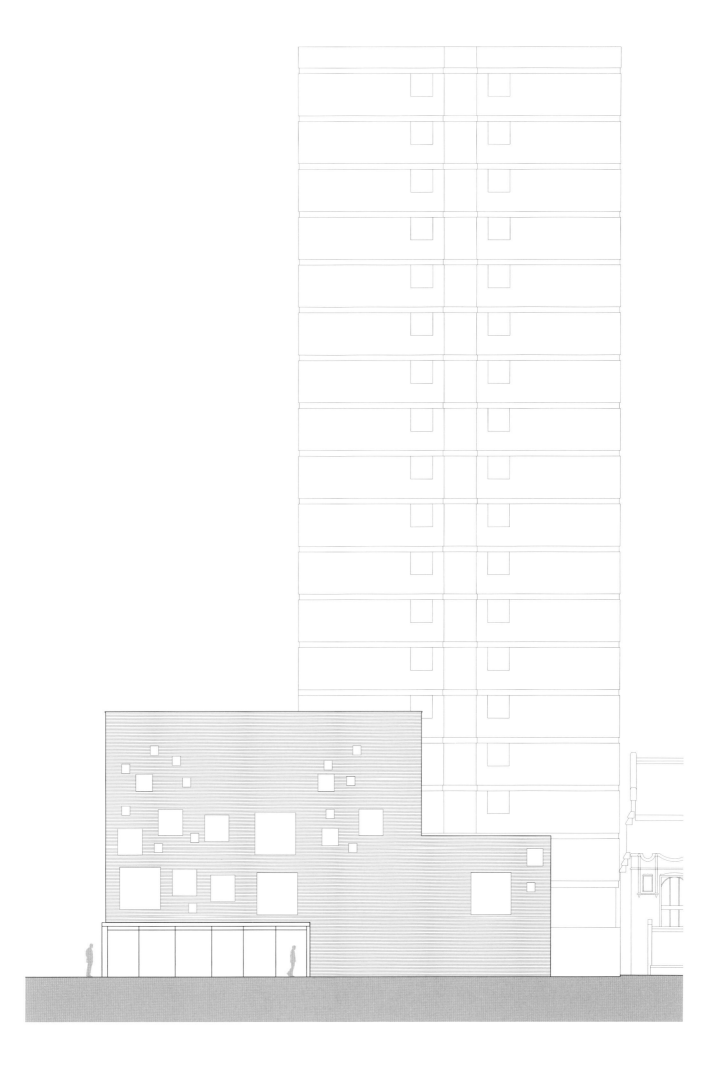

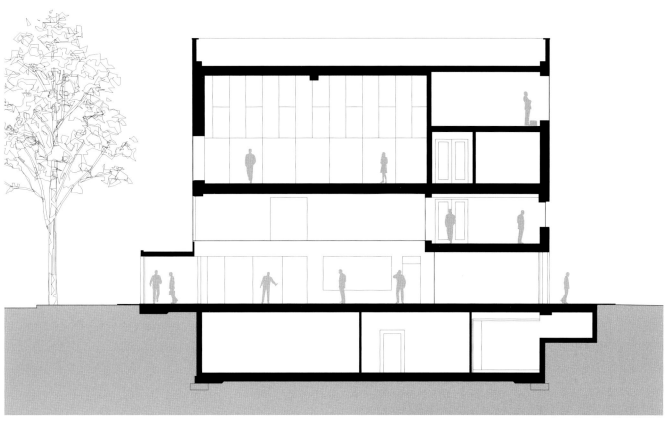

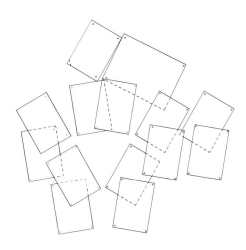

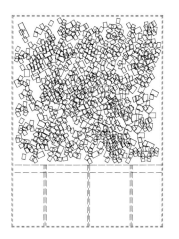

emerging architectural design. He took pictures of Nottingham's architecture – incidental moments mainly – and overlayed them onto enamel tiles, which were fixed to the ceiling in an impressive reimagining of the city's built heritage. There is also a fitting correlation with the façade's variety of window sizes, which in turn reflect the programme and the openness of the New Art Exchange as an institution. The very presence of a gallery on the ground floor lends the building a progressive character. The café may act as a draw, but the building nowhere hides its purpose as an arts centre. It has two dedicated exhibition galleries with a total floor space of 270 square metres, a performance space, a studio for an artist in residence as well as arts education work spaces shared with the local academy.

Despite the project's narrow budget, the New Art Exchange is a workable, attractive piece of architecture which meets a multitude of existing needs and is capable of adapting to more.

Opposite A composition of various-sized windows punctuate the brick façade, offering glimpses of the neighbouring context to visitors inside.

Above Section (1:200).

Left An early reflected café ceiling layout and detail of Hew Locke's installation.

Right Hew Locke's re-worked and embellished photographs of local architectural details.

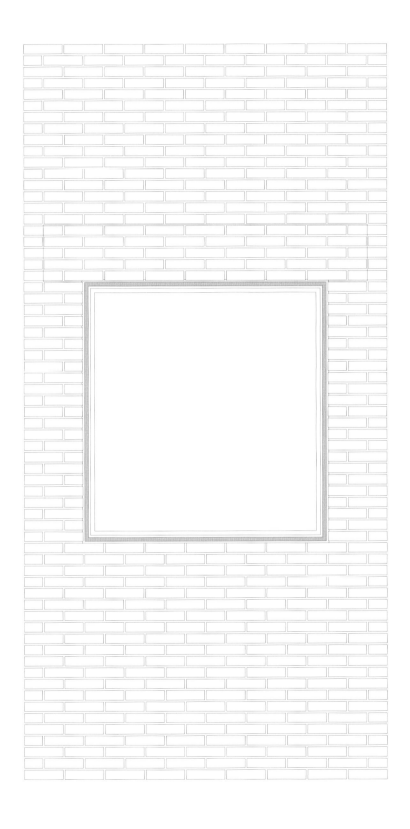

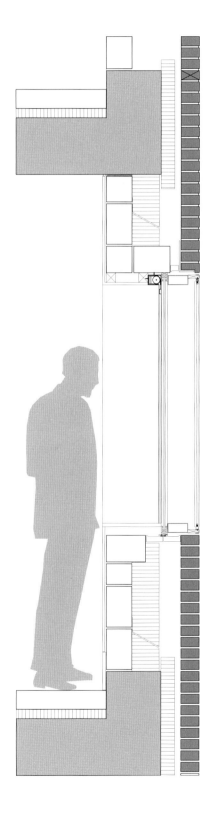

Above **Detail** (1:20).

The Roald Dahl Museum and Story Centre, Great Missenden, Buckinghamshire

Given their familiarity with the London art world, it is perhaps paradoxical that Hawkins\Brown's reputation for working in the field of the arts was originally based on redeveloping rural buildings. Yet the Henry Moore Foundation and then the Roald Dahl Museum in Great Missenden, Buckinghamshire, are both clever rationalisations of rural barns and sheds. The adroit use of robust materials, aluminium and stained wood have shown that the adaptation of rural buildings need not mean the deadening of their soul.

What makes the Roald Dahl Museum and Story Centre project so successful is not just the reorganisation of a 19th-century flint-and-brick hall and 16th-century dwellings by strategically removing some of the 20th-century additions. It is also the way that this series of spaces has been reorganised so it can display an exhibition on a remarkable writer with privileged access to both the imagination of children and the fears of adults. Dark, stained timber and reflective windows remind us of an adult's world, just as much as the segmented stable block pavers used to cover the courtyard recall the chocolate bars of Charlie and the Chocolate Factory. There is even a nod to Dahl's Norwegian heritage in the planted roofs. The practice have a created a sense that it is Dahl and not the architects who have authored the building.

Key to the manner in which Hawkins\Brown have mediated the spirit of Dahl's work is their relationship with exhibition designers Bremner & Orr, who have fashioned a narrative of Dahl's life that can expand or contract depending on the visitor's needs or wishes. The galleries are arranged in an enfilade, a planning method that allows them to be individually adjusted and remade without interrupting visitor flow. The gallery spaces too have been themed to account for different chapters in Dahl's life, and again the visitor can choose their path of investigation without the narrative being interrupted. The path through the museum culminates in a replica of the chair in which Dahl sat and wrote – the comfortable locus of his creation becomes the climax of the exhibition.

For most of us the question to what degree the past impinges on the present is a philosophical one. To the architects, though, it is pragmatic. Hawkins\Brown had to reconcile the biographical conundrum of an author in a complex of listed buildings of differing ages and provide facilities for the foundation created in his name. The architects have stripped back the architecture to its bones and celebrated the textures of the building materials in a humanistic way, showing faith in the logic of simple, architectural form and the public's ability to read it. There is no willful hierarchy to the planning, no obsessive uniformity; there is, however, a beautiful internal logic.

Above Site plan (1:2500).

Opposite above The new dark timber gallery and glazed link sit alongside the refurbished brick buildings.

Opposite below The cobbled central courtyard visually and physically connects all the functions of the museum.

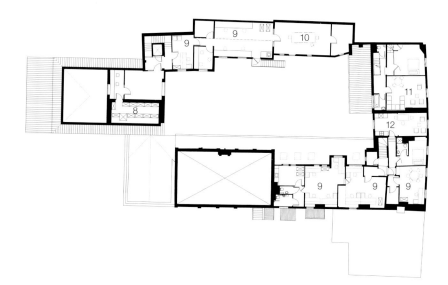

First floor plan (1:500).

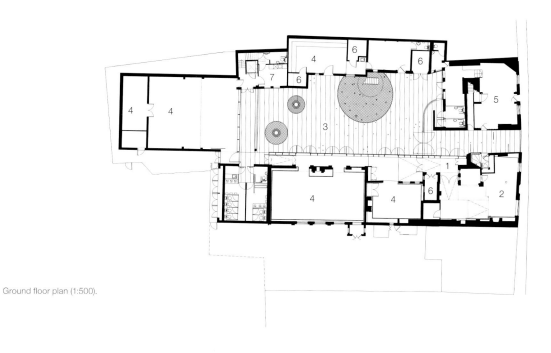

Ground floor plan (1:500).

Section (1:500).

Opposite A simple palette of
contemporary materials was chosen
to contrast with the existing listed
structure.

1 Entrance Lobby
2 Museum Shop
3 Courtyard
4 Exhibition Gallery

5 Café
6 Store
7 Staff Room
8 Archive

9 Offices
10 Meeting Room
11 Flat for Rent
12 Flat for Writer in Residence

Wysing Arts Centre, Bourn, Cambridgeshire

Wysing is nine miles west of Cambridge; it was originally a 17th-century farmhouse surrounded by the usual mixture of unremarkable, utilitarian buildings. In 1989 the site was purchased by the centre's founders, Jenny and Terry Brooks, who are still active members of the Board of Trustees, and artists Annie and Age Bunnetat. They carried out a basic conversion of the farm buildings into Wysing Arts Centre, offering low-cost studio space for artists. Hawkins\Brown had proven themselves to be adept at rationalising collections of farm buildings and turning them into arts spaces and were particularly suited to do the same at Wysing.

Hawkins\Brown's thoughtful interventions looked to rationalise the site, using development to help make sense of older converted buildings. The buildings now form a courtyard that includes a converted barn, former cowsheds, the reception buildings and a new artists' studio block that provides ten artist's spaces over two floors. The alternating rhythm of the full-height glazing and timber louvres on the front elevation make reference to the timber structure of the adjacent building, a Grade II listed farmhouse. The louvres act as part of a natural ventilation system, with internal doors that open out into the studio spaces. Internally the design strives for uncluttered simplicity, generous proportions and harnessing the use of daylight. The interior colours are restricted to white and off-white, and the concrete floors have been left bare, leaving the colour to come from the artwork in progress.

The studio block has a south-facing timber deck at first floor, which not only provides a great view of the low-lying Cambridgeshire countryside but also offers access to the studios and shade from direct sunlight. Learning from the experience at the Henry Moore Foundation and the issues of dealing with listed buildings, Hawkins\Brown decided to create two distinct structures for the buildings. This helped to maintain the intimate scale and delicate rhythm of the spaces between the farm buildings. It also emphasises the idea that Wysing is not just simply a place to consume art but a research and development centre where art is created, considered and enjoyed.

The second new structure provides a reception building and a connection to the existing gallery space. The green and yellow timber in the reception's external porch reflects the colours in the surrounding farmland. Both buildings are entirely appropriate to the location and existing structures, developing Hawkins\Brown's architectural language of buildings in the countryside seen later at Brinsbury Campus in Chichester.

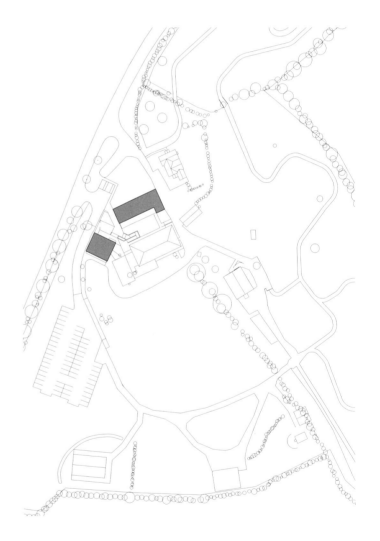

Above Site plan (1:2000).

Opposite above The new Arts Centre sits in a rural context alongside the existing 17th-century farmhouse.

Opposite below A dark-stained timber studio block sits adjacent to a vernacular reception building.

Above An external deck offers access to the studios and views across the Cambridgeshire countryside.

Below Louvered panels provide natural ventilation for the studios.

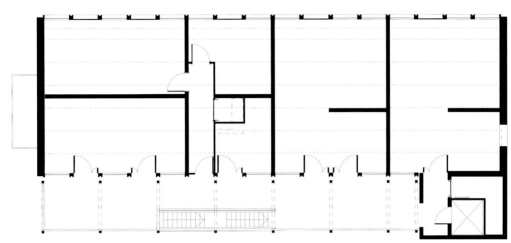

First floor plan (1:200).

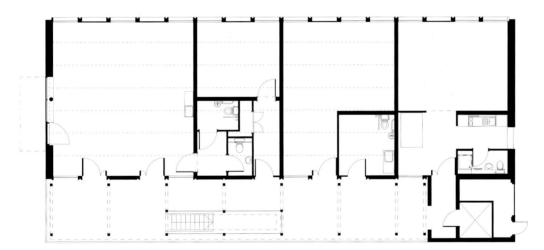

Ground floor plan (1:200).

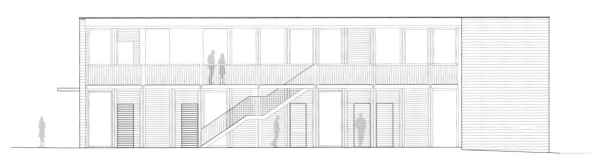

Southeast elevation (1:200).

Fourth Plinth Proposal, Trafalgar Square, Westminster, London

For architects to collaborate regularly with artists there has to be something more than a shared professional goal and a shared aesthetic sensitivity. There also needs to be some understanding or involvement in the informal social networks of the art world. David Bickle's relationship with Patrick Brill, a.k.a Bob and Roberta Smith, is a case in point. As Jes Fernie points out in her essay in this book, Hawkins\Brown originally came into contact with the artist through a competition to design a new town square for Hackney. Their 'I Believe In Hackney' project emerged from an appreciation of Bob and Roberta Smith's 'I Believe in' works which he was making separately around the same time and combining it with the thinking behind Glasgow's 'Miles Better Campaign'.

They were brought back in touch by the 'Art U Need' project, an ambitious programme of artworks led by Bob and Roberta Smith which were to transform public, open spaces in the Thames Gateway in 2006. Smith had invited fellow artist Jane Wilbraham to work in Purfleet. Wilbraham in turn knew Hawkins\Brown from their work at Hales Gallery, and the friends spoke about practical issues related to the construction of her giant 'Trojan Fish' which toured around as the 'Purfleet One Float Carnival'. While watching the float travel through the coastal Essex town, David Bickle met Bob and Roberta Smith again; it was then that he mentioned that he had just been shortlisted in the competition to fill the Fourth Plinth in Trafalgar Square. Built in 1841, the Fourth Plinth was originally intended for an equestrian statue but has been empty since. It is now the location for specially commissioned artworks which take on national significance.

David Bickle offered to provide structural and environmental engineering expertise to Smith, who had proposed a sculpture called 'Faites L'Art Pas La Guerre', an illuminated peace sign powered by the wind and sun. Smith liked the drawings of the bare engineered version of his work more than his own sketches and maquettes. As an architect, Bickle had sought to make a simplified version of the assemblage in order "to make clear the structure of the sculpture", but to Smith the power of Bickle's design sketches lay in their ability to let viewers experience a poetic quality inherent in the revealed structure.

This collaboration is not only an example of Hawkins\Brown's relationship with the art world and their commitment to the kind of art they admire, but it is also a sign of the aesthetic values and social vision they share. Bickle describes Smith as an "open and honest communicator, perhaps the best communicator I've worked with. Capable of exploring the absurdities and contradictions of life without offending people."

Above Bob and Roberta Smith stands alongside a scale model of his proposal.

Opposite 'Faites L'Art Pas La Guerre' (make art, not war), a peace sign powered by the wind and the sun.

Sevenstone New Retail Quarter, Sheffield

Within the masterplan for the Sevenstone development in Sheffield, Hawkins\Brown were given a triangular site of existing Edwardian buildings, previously used as shops and flats. The block is largely going to be demolished although the apex of the site and an Edwardian façade needed to be retained to satisfy planning conditions. The challenge was how to integrate an existing façade of this kind into a new retail development. The discussion within the studio focused on using gothic Victorian ornament to evoke certain historical memories. Sarah Staton was introduced to Hawkins\Brown as an artist who could develop an appropriate decorative language to reinforce the architectural ideas.

Incorporating the retained building with the new structures posed a particular problem: the floor levels of the new development behind the existing façade were dictated by commercial requirements and did not match those of the Edwardian building. In some cases the new floor plates will run behind existing window openings. To disguise this, Staton suggested the insertion of a layer of tile panels which evoked Victorian tiled public buildings like the original London Underground stations. These interventions will reinforce the spirit of the façade's diaper brickwork and maintain the rhythm and geometry of its composition. The tile pattern resembles a Victorian sampler, set out like a cross-stitch pattern. The pixelated design makes reference to the geometry of the brickwork in the new façades, so that it establishes a harmony with the rest of the scheme. Behind the outer layer of glass panels, reflective linings provide a sparkle that literally reflects to the glass façade of the project by Foreign Office Architects immediately opposite.

Sarah Staton also suggested exaggerating the mansard roofs, which is one of the most striking aspects of the completed design. Thanks in part to her contribution, the project creates a link between Sheffield's trades, past and present. The concept of filling in the windows in an innovative way and playing with the Victorian heritage of the block means that the cultural context is reinforced.

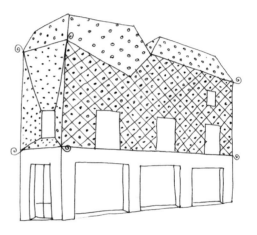

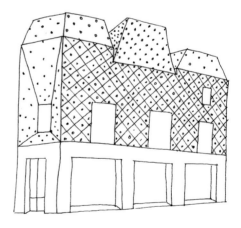

Above Sketches by Sarah Staton exploring the potential for an exaggerated mansard roof.

Opposite above Sketch by Sarah Staton of the pattern for the window infills.

Opposite below The final proposal.

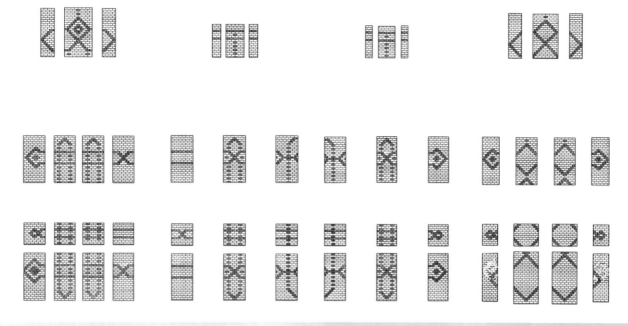

Tottenham Court Road Station Upgrade, London

Tottenham Court Road is one of the British capital's busiest tube stations. Not only does it stand at the east end of Oxford Street, but it is a transfer between the busy Central Line and the Northern Line. Originally the stations were separate, but in the 1920s they became one awkward, frequently congested station. The Northern Line is deep underground, and its platforms only have a single means of escape rather than two required by modern legislation. In the light of the fire at King's Cross station in 1987 it became a priority to solve this problem.

The much-needed upgrade to Tottenham Court Road tube station finally went on site in May 2009, 17 years after Hawkins\ Brown were first given the commission. The work involves the complete reimagining of this multiple interchange station. The current cramped ticket hall will be raised and expanded to five times its current size. Daylight will be introduced through a huge rooflight and new entrances created at street level.

Placing art in such a context is no easy feat. But given the fact that the station is home to what is perhaps the most beautiful artwork on the Underground, Eduardo Paolozzi's friezes, it was a challenge that the client as much as the architect wished to continue. Daniel Buren was chosen from 15 artists, sourced by Art on the Underground. This body ensures that the London Underground is a complex network of challenging, progressive art sites as well as an immense subterranean rail network. Buren is still perhaps best known for his *Deux Plateaux* installations in the courtyard of the Palais-Royal in Paris in 1986, which upset traditionalists across Europe.

For Hawkins\Brown it was important that Buren's work is always site specific, and invariably uses art as a means of manipulating our understanding of space rather than altering the space in itself. One of Buren's earliest projects was the clandestine posting of hundreds of striped posters in the Paris metro stations. At Tottenham Court Road, Buren, now an established artist, is returning to the underground, but now he has an architect who he regularly works with to lay out his striped pieces on glass.

Perhaps the biggest and ultimately highest profile collaboration with an artist is inevitably more formal. The relationship with Buren is the same as it would be with the company that installs the glazing. Yet for Roger Hawkins, the collaboration is still alive with possibility. "Buren's perception of space is much more refined. He's willing to accommodate other needs and he really understands the building process and architecture," he says.

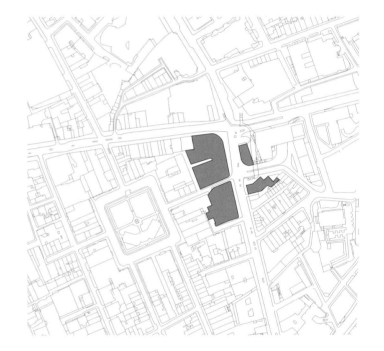

Above **Site plan** (1:5000).

Indeed for a practice like Hawkins\Brown, which have not consciously developed a signature style, the result of the collaboration with Buren points at one of the recurring themes. Pattern, particularly pattern which expresses or is responsive to movement, is a leitmotif that emerges time and again in the work of Hawkins\Brown. The New Biochemistry building at Oxford, to provide an example, is panelled with seven different coloured glass panels on the façade, a combination that picks up the rhythm of a pedestrian walking around it. Buren's work at Tottenham Court Road operates on a similar way – a means of complimenting and commenting on the throng that will pass through the Underground station when, some two decades after the decision to rebuild it, it will finally open.

Left Artwork by Daniel Buren will be encapsulated within the internal glass wall cladding.

Above Internal view of the new ticket hall.

Next page The upgraded station entrance will feature colourful artworks by Daniel Buren.

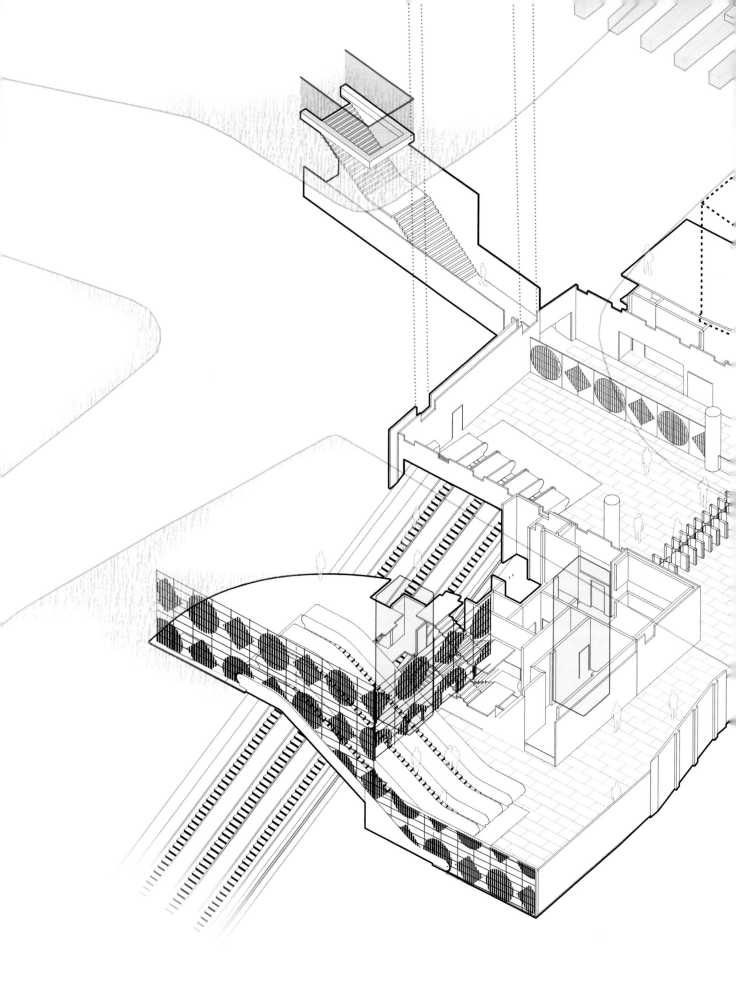

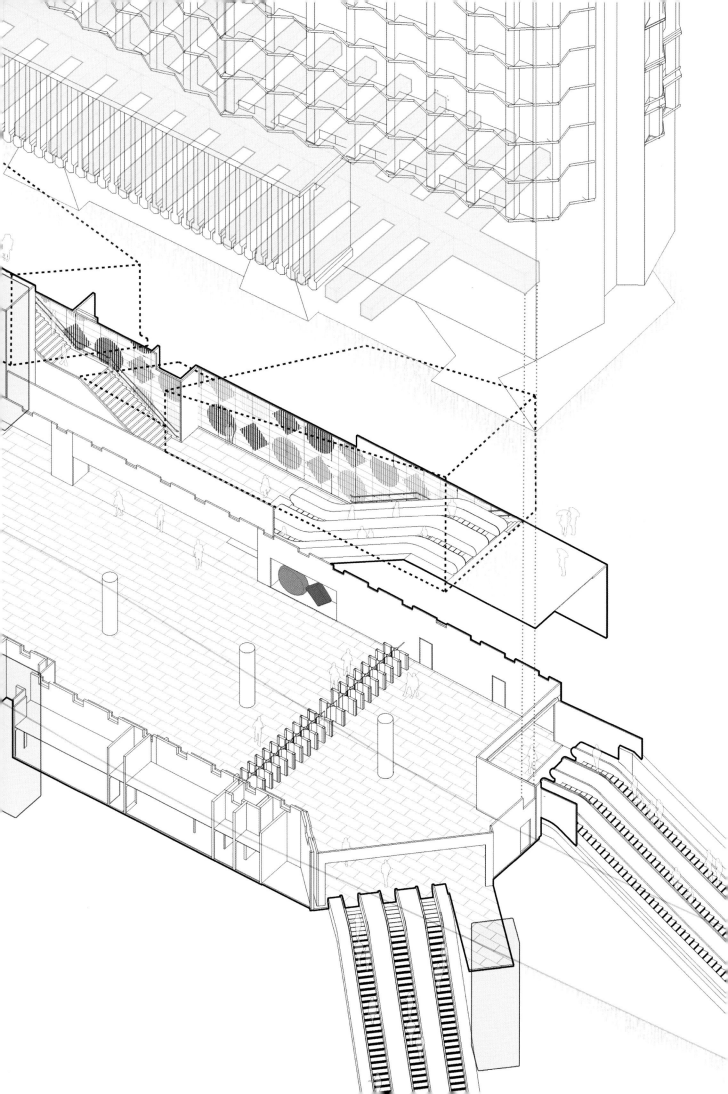

The Henry Moore Foundation, Perry Green, Hertfordshire

In Henry Moore's final years, his international reputation was built into the urban fabric of Leeds, his home town. In 1986, a new wing, largely funded by the Henry Moore Foundation, was built onto the back of the city's art gallery. Dixon and Jones refurbished three 19th-century warehouses for the Henry Moore Institute, covering a blank gable end with polished black granite slabs, thus memorialising the important role the artist played in British cultural life.

Perry Green is 170 miles south of Leeds. It is where Henry Moore worked for over 40 years, moving there in 1940 to escape the Blitz and then slowly taking over various farm buildings for studios, workshops and storage. As Moore's reputation grew, so did his estate. When he died in 1986, it was proposed that a public gallery be built at Perry Green, conceived in the tradition of the European state gallery. This huge gallery – half cultural institution, half memorial – was hotly contested by local people and did not receive planning permission. During a chance meeting with the curator David Mitchinson, he explained to Roger Hawkins that a planning permission already existed for incremental changes to the amalgam of converted farm buildings and that this could be a way to move forward with the project.

Thus Hawkins\Brown's relationship with artists began with the patrimony of the most influential figure in 20th-century British art. The relationship with the Henry Moore Foundation evolved in a phase when this organisation with an international reputation was still unsure of its relationship to its neighbours in Perry Green. Over 12 years and five phases, Hawkins\Brown have helped turn the Henry Moore Foundation from an inward-looking base for conservation into a public arts facility of national significance.

The first step was the extension of the archive and secure store at Dane Tree House: providing storage for maquettes and works on paper, and most strikingly opening up the upper floor of the building with glazing to allow light to flood into the workshops and research areas.

The second step was the remodelling of an early 20th-century house on the edge of the site, to create new entrances and reception areas to Dane Tree House.

Their most significant project at Perry Green was the Sheep Field Barn Gallery completed in 1999. The new building re-used the steel frame of a second-hand agricultural barn, which Moore had bought and sited himself. He used one third of the building to store hay and the remainder for sculpture packing crates. Hawkins\Brown completely restructured the building, giving it a

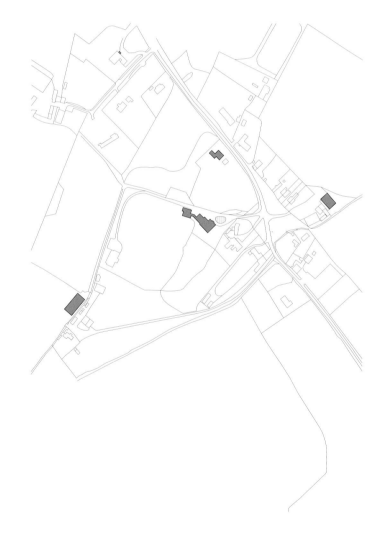

A collection of new buildings sit within the estate where Henry Moore lived and practiced.

zinc roof and a base of Staffordshire blue brick. Picking up on the black-stained weather-boarding used around the site, and across the south of England, they designed black timber panels which recall the packing crates in which Moore's work was transported around the world. The new building's interior provides a lofty top-lit sculpture space and a gallery with controlled daylight for the display of delicate artefacts and works on paper.

Over nearly ten years Hawkins\Brown have quietly transformed Moore's studios into a place were the artist's practice can be explored and brought back to life.

Above The Sheep Field Barn Gallery completed for the millennium sits alongside monumental sculptures set within the landscape.

Below The Sheep Field Barn Gallery is used to display small sculptures and works on paper.

Artists Studio and Apartment, Tower Hamlets, London

The Bethnal Green Great Synagogue was founded in 1906. It was rebuilt after it was destroyed in the Blitz, but it closed in 1966. The life story of the building is almost exactly contiguous with the trajectory of the Jewish community in the East End of London. The majority of immigrants came from Eastern Europe at the turn of the century and left to the suburbs of north London in the 1960s. The synagogue was bought by Rachel Whiteread, an artist who has memorialised the history of the East End in her famous project *House* (1993) where she made a cast of the interior of a terraced house and exhibited it on the site of the original. Whiteread's work has also frequently addressed the Jewish experience during the Second World War. At the time when she moved into the synagogue in Bethnal Green she had just completed the Holocaust Memorial in the Judenplatz in Vienna, also known as the Nameless Library.

In their redesign of the synagogue, Hawkins\Brown divided the main ceremonial space horizontally, providing a workshop for manufacturing, casting and making. Above, two separate studio spaces were inserted; one for Whiteread and another for her partner Marcus Taylor, who is also an artist. Taylor uses his space for making maquettes and drawings. New guest accommodation was inserted onto the same floor. Above this, on top of the old roof, Hawkins\Brown built two pavilions, one to the east containing a library and another to the west containing kitchen and living areas; both with glazed doors facing towards each other which could be retracted. In between is a roof terrace, which has since had a conservatory added to it in order to connect the two pavilions.

Much of the effort put into this redesign came in the sensitive way Hawkins\Brown related the renovation of the building to Whiteread's own practice. An example is the precision casting of a reinforced concrete stair that links the studio to the library floor. The upper pavilions were clad in a cementitious board, giving it the texture of Whiteread's precast sculptures. Given her strong interest in memorials, a great deal of time was spent deliberating whether the Star of David should be retained on the busy street elevation, whilst the original stained glass windows were crated and incarcerated within the new mezzanine floor construction, and could be reinstated at some future date. The new point of entry is orientated away from the synagogue's main entrance, as Whiteread felt uncomfortable walking through such a ceremonial entrance. Issues of privacy related to Whiteread's public status as a famous artist reinforced this decision. At the time of construction, this was the first building of its kind in a dilapidated area of East London. Now Whiteread's house is next door to David Adjaye's house for Noble and Webster and at the heart of a thriving arts quarter.

Above The existing synagogue before conversion.   Below The finished building.

South elevation (1:200).

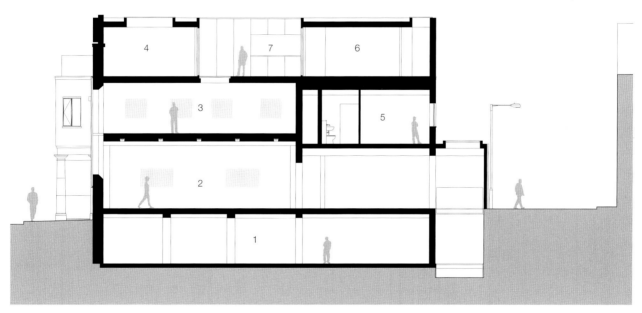

Section (1:200).

1 Archive
2 Sculpture Studio
3 Drawing Studio
4 Library
5 Bedroom
6 Living Room
7 External Terrace

124\ Collaborating with Designers

Writing on the Wall
by Erik Spiekermann

The relationship between graphic designers and architects has never been one of equals. This is not surprising, as architecture is one of the oldest professions and the physical environment is less transient than the published word. Although it was not until the 19th century that the architect's work was fully recognised as a profession, the role of building designer has ancient roots. Graphic design, on the other hand, is not even 100 years old. The term was first coined by the American artist William Addison Dwiggins in 1922 to describe his various activities, like book design, illustration, typography, lettering and calligraphy. It did not become customary to speak of graphic design as a separate role until after the Second World War.

Dwiggins was a commercial artist. One could accuse him of self-promotion when he described himself as a graphic designer. What is more interesting is that most of the other early graphic designers started out as architects, and they, in turn, were often influenced by artists. The German architect and designer Peter Behrens is considered the first industrial designer. In 1907 he was retained by AEG (Allgemeine Elektricitäts-Gesellschaft) in Berlin as artistic consultant. He was responsible for the entire 'look' of the company: buildings, products, logo, typeface and publicity. The term corporate identity had not yet been coined, but effectively that is what Behrens was concerned with; this made him the first corporate designer.

Behrens' appointment by AEG was a landmark as for the first time a manufacturer, particularly a large one, had hired and developed an alliance with an artist to advise on all facets of industrial design. He is primarily remembered for his role as their architect. For a time in 1910, Behrens had Le Corbusier, Walter Gropius and Mies van der Rohe working for him at the same time. However, his work in graphics was hugely influential. His book *Feste des Lebens und der Kunst: Eine Betrachtung des Theaters als höchsten Kultursymbols* (Celebrations of life and art: a consideration of the theatre as the highest symbol of culture) is believed to be the first use of sans serif type as running book text. At the time he wrote that, after architecture, typography provided "the most characteristic picture of a period and the strongest testimonial of the spiritual progress [and] development of a people".

Laying out a page said as much about a culture as laying out a city. Incorporating the work of the Dutch architect J.L.M. Lauweriks, Behrens proposed teaching all facets of design based on geometric composition. His grids began with a square inscribed with a circle, and the subsequent permutations were made possible by subdividing and duplicating this basic structure. This approach was disseminated to pupils at the Düsseldorf School of Arts and Craft where he was director from 1903. Even before he gave them work at AEG, this course became a training ground for influential modernists like Mies van der Rohe and Walter Gropius. These architects went on to start the Bauhaus school in 1919, where again we see architecture and graphic design closely linked. One of the most influential teachers at the school was El Lissitzky. He trained as an architect but started his career illustrating childrens' books. His work marked the beginning of a new graphic art by showing how art could be used as a powerful means of visual communication. His relationship with Walter Gropius and Jan Tschichold resulted in a radical rethinking of graphic art. El Lissitzky also influenced the De Stijl movement.

Architects like Gerrit Rietveld applied De Stijl's principles of pure geometry to furniture and buildings. Piet Zwart, on the other hand, went from graphics to designing furniture, products and interiors after he had been the most influential Dutch graphic designer of the 1920s and 30s. He constructed his pages, using primary colours, geometric elements and photographs; so the step to making objects in three dimensions was like freeing himself from the constraints of two dimensions.

In Britain, modernist principles were applied in a less radical manner. Edward Johnstone's signage for the London Underground did not shock anybody at the time, even though he used a sans serif typeface, the hallmark of modernist typography. He designed

Hawkins/Brown Issue 3-Public Realm
Illustration by Adam Pointer

60

his alphabet for the Underground, based on vernacular and industrial typography of the late 19th century, in 1916, well before Paul Renner's Futura was even thought of. Like Renner, Johnstone stripped the letters of superfluous embellishments but kept their classic Roman proportions. That made it acceptable to modernist architects.

Futura was the 'Type of our Times', based on drawings by the architect Ferdinand Kramer. He worked with Ernst May on The New Frankfurt project, developing a large-scale housing programme between 1925 and 1930. Margarete Schütte-Lihotzky's Frankfurt Kitchen was installed in some 10,000 of these homes. This became the prototype of the modern 'built-in' kitchen, based on her idea that "housing is the organized implementation of living habits".

The booming post-war economy needed graphic design, especially in the USA. Advertising and packaging were the main applications for this new profession. The emigration of European designers brought modernist design theories to the USA. László Moholy-Nagy founded the New Bauhaus School of Design in Chicago in 1937 and developed the curriculum originally devised by Walter Gropius for the original Bauhaus, which had been dissolved in 1933 under Nazi pressure.

American graphic designer, Paul Rand, was more or less self-taught, learning about the works of the great European designers from the pages of magazines like *Gebrauchsgraphik* (Applied graphic design). He created corporate identities for companies like IBM, UPS and Westinghouse, as well as his own company when he changed his name from the overtly Jewish Peretz Rosenbaum to his new brand of 'Four plus four letters'. Rand's primary talent was his ability to present and explain his work to large corporations. He convinced business that design was an effective tool and gave the new profession credibility.

The need to announce products and services in magazines, newspapers, TV ads and on the high-streets or shopping malls brought a lot of work to these new consultancies. International advertising agencies, of mostly US origin, usually employed hundreds of copywriters and graphic artists ('creatives', as they were called) next to their account executives and media buyers. By the early 1960s, graphic design studios in the US had reached the size of architectural studios and rivalled them for the scope of their budgets and the attention of clients.

Designing for brands has become big business. Design companies are often part of international networks that include advertising, packaging, PR, multimedia, online – new names for new skills are being added all the time. When companies or institutions mention the word architecture, they will often be talking about 'brand architecture' – where services, products and sub-brands come together under one umbrella brand.

'Corporate architecture' may well be part of what brand consultancies (as some graphic design firms now call themselves) define as being an important facet of a company's image. Architects will be asked to work within the constraints of these brand guidelines. The division between the work of retail designers, interior designers, exhibition designers and 'proper' architects can become blurred, as design consultancies employ traditionally-trained architects next to the other 'creatives'. Companies like Imagination can offer the full spectrum of services their clients often do not know they need.

Graphic design as a profession has benefited from our world becoming more complex, and some people will say it has been compromised by its blurring with advertising and brand development. The only good thing about graphic designers is that nothing they do will last, or so they say. Whatever pages, screens or walls they cover with their messages will soon be reprinted, repainted or reprogrammed. Who reads yesterday's paper? Architects are also getting used to providing more short-term image adjustments when they are called in to improve the image of a company or a whole town. This 'gehryfication' is something graphic designers have been doing since the profession was invented.

There are, of course, designers who work with hard-core information like unemployment forms, factual websites or complex wayfinding systems. They understand that they cannot solve a problem without adding the 10% of aesthetics that the Swiss architect and designer Max Bill demanded. Neither can they simply make beautiful images without making the information therein accessible. Some graphic designers have even managed to work with architects. Unfortunately, architects often consider a building signage as an annoying distraction from the building itself and will never engage a graphic designer to lay-out their coffee-table books. Most of the books published by architectural practices remain square and impossible to hold with long lines set in modernist sans serif typefaces, as tightly spaced as possible and thus illegible. And graphic designers will carry on thinking that it is enough to buy some 3-d software in order to design spaces by simply adding the z-axis.

Opposite The Hawkins\Brown Studio, 60 Bastwick Street, London.

Hawkins\Brown and SEA have brought the two disciplines into a creative partnership. The architects have introduced the graphic designers to their clients to help manage a brand (at Metropolitan Wharf), conceive signage for a new public building (Corby Cube) or design their own corporate brand. The graphic designers bring their architect friends along to give physical form to the new corporate structures that spin out of new brands and new thinking.

Hawkins\Brown and SEA enjoy their time together, John Simpson (from SEA) and David Bickle sparking off ideas, bouncing between the world of images and words, and the outlines of new places and spaces.

Opposite The entrance window features a specially commissioned graphic by Adam Pointer.

Wellesley Road and Park Lane Masterplan, Croydon, London

In 1998 the London Borough of Croydon produced a planning strategy, which was subsequently developed by Alsop Architects into the 'Third City Plan'. An international urban design competition for a major part of this plan, Wellesley Road and Park Lane, was launched in October 2008. These main roads currently make up an urban motorway dominated by 1960s underpasses and subways. Effectively this cuts the heart of the town in two, forming a physical barrier to easy movement running east-west. The competition was to transform this into a 1.5 kilometre stretch of the public realm in central Croydon. Hawkins\Brown were one of four design teams shortlisted from over 50 submissions.

The new design had to reverse the original planning emphasis on the car. The key challenge was to reduce the main arterial traffic route down from an eight-lane highway to two lanes of traffic with bus and tram. The scheme was looking for an overarching urban design strategy for public spaces that would result in the two halves of the town being stitched back together. Hawkins\Brown's scheme used landscape interventions to slow air and reduce noise along the length of the road. Pockets of woodland offered mitigation as wind baffles, reducing the winds that affect this open stretch of road. These pockets of woodland would introduce a new ecosystem into the heart of suburban Croydon.

The 'stitching together' became a metaphor and presentational theme for the scheme, making analogies with fashion and tailoring. Indeed Croydon's most illustrious ex-residents, Kate Moss, Malcolm McLaren and Bridget Riley, all have a relationship with fashion. An intense collaboration with Grant Associates on landscape, Max Fordham for sustainability, Jason Bruges Studio on lighting and branding advice from SEA Design and Squint/Opera, created a unique urban design scheme that was presented as a sewn and stitched fabric plan of the proposals.

Although Hawkins\Brown were unsuccessful in winning the first competition, the team won a subsequent competition to work on an important part of the wider masterplan. With Studio Egret West as partners they will design an expansion of East Croydon station, adding platforms and building a new bridge over the railway and then integrating an extended station with bus and tram terminuses.

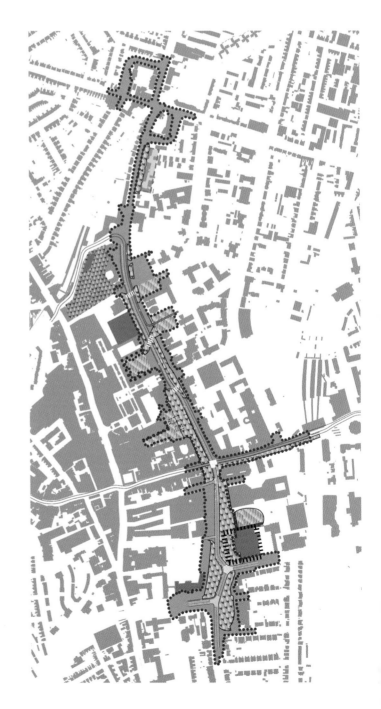

Right The overall masterplan covered a stretch of over 1.5 kilometres of the city centre.

Opposite Metaphors of tailoring, stitching and weaving were drawn out through this maquette, a textile version of the proposals.

Above The maquette, under construction.

Below A suite of four bespoke scarves was made to reflect geometric patterns from the context, Croydon's punk history, and to link in with the movie made by Squint/Opera.

Opposite above The design was to be the green lung of the city, with urban atomisers to de-pollute, moisten and fragrance the air.

Opposite below 'Shibuya Croydon', a major pedestrian crossing in the proposals, is designed as a Japanese style 'scramble' junction.

WILDLIFE
CONNECTIONS FOR
INSECTS
AND BIRDS

NOBLE OAKS AND
MAJESTIC BEECH

URBAN
ATOMISER

NATURE'S
ATOMISER

Where City .... meets Country

BEEP

BEEP

BEEP

BEEP

BEEP

BEEP

BEEP

BEEP

GEORGE STREET

STOP

136\
70 St Johns Street, Islington, London

Hawkins\Brown became aware of SEA Design when they were working for the Architecture Foundation, who were subtenants in their Bastwick Street studio. At that time, David Bickle became interested in the graphic design of the brochures that SEA produced for exhibitions curated by the Architecture Foundation. It was only in 1999 that the two practices began working together, when SEA bought offices at 70 St. John Street, close to Hawkins\Brown. The former engineering works, which became known affectionately as 'SEA Towers', was fitted out with design advice from Hawkins\Brown.

SEA use the ground floor for display and exhibitions. One of the most memorable shows was an exhibition that they put together with Hawkins\Brown and the writer Pete Kirby for the first London Architecture Biennale in 2004. It was called 'House\Home' and examined the way that items like cat flaps, loft ladders, garden sheds, doorknockers, the rotary clothes dryer, milkman's mates, etc. are excluded from briefs for new housing. Such omissions forfeit opportunities for neighbourly conviviality and the extended activities of hobbies, pets, letting clothes dry by the wind or finding new places to store the Christmas decorations.

The relationship established between the two studios has been incredibly productive and SEA have contributed to most of Hawkins\Brown's significant projects. One of the first projects where the architects suggested SEA as graphic designers and communicators was The Corner, a straightforward renovation of a Clerkenwell office block. It was SEA's branding that lifted this project out of the ordinary. At present SEA are providing a brand identity and graphics for Corby Cube, the Aldingbourne Trust and the Student Enterprise Building at Coventry University and are in the process of designing books that feature Hawkins\Brown's work.

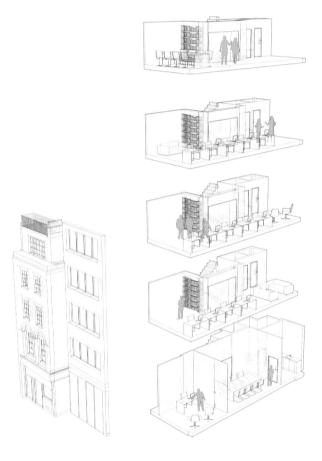

Above **The proposal for SEA Design's refurbished office featured new meeting rooms at ground floor where currently an open plan studio lies in disuse.**

Opposite above **In 2004 Hawkins\Brown staged an exhibition as part of the Clerkenwell Biennale.**

Opposite below left **SEA Design's 'House\Home' exhibition catalogue.**

Opposite below right **The exhibition features nostalgic graphics of familiar 'homely' objects.**

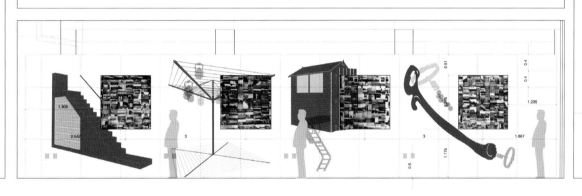

OQO,
Islington, London

When Hawkins\Brown met Mark Chan, he was a consultant urologist with the ambition to open a cocktail bar. He had the idea for a place which would serve all-day Chinese dim sum to accompany the exotic cocktails that he created. It was a great idea, similar to the one which the bar and restaurant chain Ping Pong turned into a major success. At the time Chan did not even have a name for this new business. It was clear to Hawkins\Brown that he not only needed help to imagine the architecture of his restaurant but also the vision of it as a brand so they suggested SEA Design become involved.

Firstly, SEA came up with the name OQO, and the logo then became a major element of the interior: huge photographs of circular slices of fruit and cocktail glasses decorate the walls, as well as luscious close-ups of the food. Because the budget could not stretch to high-quality finishes, the pictures were hot-press laminated onto the wall. Tablemats, tables, coasters and seating were created in shapes and colours inspired by SEA's logo design. To allow the graphics to stand out, Hawkins\Brown covered the rest of the interior in black, including the ceilings.

Indeed, the minimal architectural interventions and the dark backgrounds emphasised the luminous qualities of the supersized graphics. A single stretch of backlit perspex reaches along the length of the bar, providing the space's solitary destination. In the toilets, backlit corrugated plastic walls were superimposed with the outline of male and female symbols.

As part of Hawkins\Brown's output, OQO and Scin (see page 140) may not seem significant. But the understanding of the building types developed through these projects has fed into other, larger schemes. At Corby Cube, the idea of a single megastructure containing a host of civic and cultural functions could only be effective with a graphic approach that went beyond simple way-finding to reinforcing the building's unifying concept. A similar graphic logic has been applied to the Drama and Visual Arts building at the University of Kent. In these projects, there is very little difference between graphic design, interior design and architecture. For Hawkins\Brown, they represent an inspiring blurring of visual languages as the basis for a successful creative partnership.

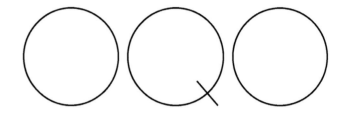

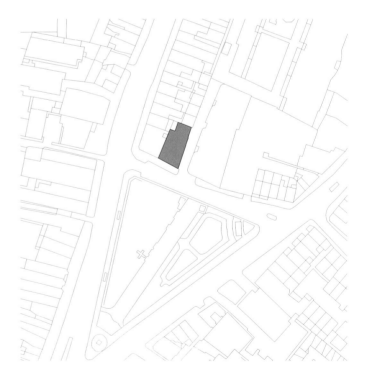

Above OQO logo by SEA Design.
Below Site plan (1:2000).

Opposite A holistic approach to branding was taken, blending text and graphics into the entrance, the matchstick packaging and the interior.

4–6 ISLINGTON GREEN
LONDON N1 2XA
T 020 7704 2332
F 020 7704 2339
WWW.OQOBAR.CO.UK

Scin,
Notting Hill, London

Of all the multifarious projects that Hawkins\Brown have been involved in, from massive engineering schemes for Crossrail to art buildings in rural Hertfordshire, perhaps the most singular are two interior projects: one for a restaurant/bar, the other is a beauty spa. And yet, this work has helped cement the important relationship with the graphic designers SEA. Invited to design a prototype spa in London's fashionable Notting Hill, Hawkins\Brown realised that the client was having difficulty with creating a coherent brand to link all their associated products and merchandise and introduced them to SEA.

The physical spa and the brand itself are virtually indistinguishable. Taking the graphic designers' fat, lower-case serif rendering of the adapted spelling of 'skin' one can see how it helped the architects establish the right mix of purity and comfort in their design. The bespoke font created for the brand name is reminiscent of Cooper Black. Created in the 1920s, this font has that era's rigour, but was popularised by the psychedelic posters of the late 1960s and 70s. SEA's font has the same flowing outer contours that create both muscular and soft forms. Rendered in white on a white background on the outside of the building, this contrasts with the ornate marble cornices of the shop front to communicate a feeling of luxury, body forms and health.

Hawkins\Brown took this as a starting point to create a design that is both pure and cosily immersive. The teardrop lighting in the shop windows echoes the forms of the logo. To offset the clinical connotations of the white interiors in the beauty treatment room, they added more comfortable elements such as quilted seating. In the spirit of the profusion of warm Mediterranean colours the low-level coloured lighting in the spa itself contrasts with the cool ambience of the treatment areas.

Above Scin logo by SEA Design.
Below Site plan (1:2000).

Opposite A tranquil palette of whites and blues was chosen and complemented by subtle grey text.

Metropolitan Wharf, Tower Hamlets, London

The riverside warehouses of London have been so exhaustively plundered for conversion into residential properties that it is surprising to know that there are any left. It is even more surprising to learn that Metropolitan Wharf in Wapping is being redeveloped so sensitively. Nick Capstick-Dale of UK Real Estate clearly has an eye to creating a viable community of mixed and vibrant uses. Hawkins\Brown's involvement with the site predates the current owners. They were initially appointed to renovate the six-storey riverside building by Capital and Counties. It was so run-down that the only people who rented the office and studio spaces were architects and designers.

The redevelopment of Wapping has created a mono-culture of wealthy flat owners who work in nearby Canary Wharf or the City and who frequently return to a rural family house at the weekends. As a result, Wapping is usually an eerie place outside working hours. Reacting rather late to this effect, Tower Hamlets has tried to address the problem by insisting on the retention of employment space, in redeveloped buildings. Accordingly, Capital and Counties had been turned down when it tried to obtain planning permission to turn the whole building into residential units. They held on to Metropolitan Wharf for over a decade with little investment before Hawkins\Brown became involved. From 2006 to 2008, the architects connected together disjointed floor plates, opened up views from the roadside through to the river and repaired much of the masonry, roofing and brickwork. In 2009 the building was acquired by UK Real Estate.

The new owner had long been an admirer of the building and had tried to buy it on a number of previous occasions. Hawkins\Brown found that as a partner in the private arts club Soho House, they had a much richer appreciation of the potential of Metropolitan Wharf. They were very interested in their ideas for multiple uses, cultural re-programming and rebranding the building as an Urban Village.

Nick Capstick-Dale clearly has a desire to maintain a hold on the look and feel of the building, an attitude the architects greatly appreciate, as they now have an enthusiastic collaborator in their ideas. The new owner is looking for a way of creating an individual identity for small businesses working within a huge building. With six floors and eight units on each floor, an overall design strategy was needed to make these differences. Longtime collaborators SEA Design pitched on Hawkins\

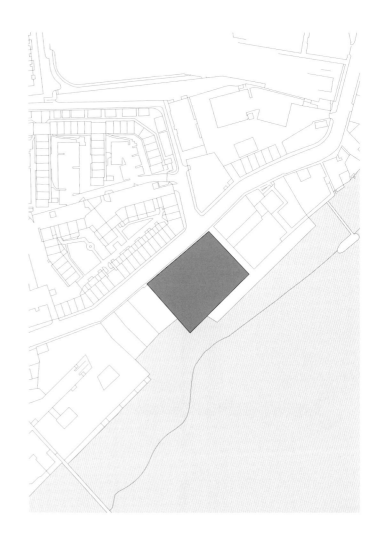

Above Site plan (1:2500).

Opposite above Built as a goods warehouse in the late 19th century, and now Grade II listed, Metropolitan Wharf had fallen into a state of disrepair until 2005.

Opposite below Following refurbishment, the building will now house a vibrant mix of uses.

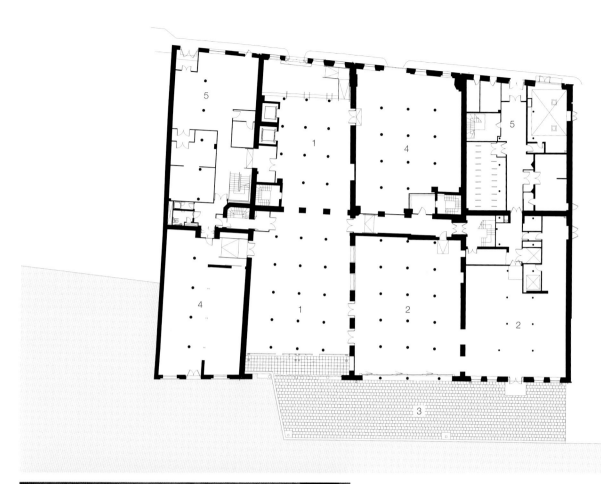

Brown's recommendation and will create a brand identity for the whole enterprise. It uses a new font based on the lettering on the roof of the building. This font will be employed in signage through the building and will be extended through all the web and print-based publicity materials.

The new owner is set on the idea of the building as village in and of itself – a refreshing decision given that the Wapping area has been built almost exclusively for residential use and as such has little or no atmosphere. This presents a challenge for making the building legible for the visitor, however. Katie Tonkinson believes that the distinctive graphics developed by SEA can be used in the architectural design for "guiding tenants, occupants and visitors around". The creation of a single unified design from multiple uses is only achievable if close collaboration, with graphic designers as with others, begins at an early stage.

Opposite A sensitively pragmatic approach to conserving the building's historic character was taken. Bricks were cleaned and only replaced where necessary, creating a patchwork of the old and the new.

Above Ground floor plan (1:500).
1 Reception Area
2 Riverside Restaurant
3 Pier
4 Retail
5 Back of House

Middle The reconfigured ground floor makes a strong connection between the street and the river.

Below New elements of circulation are raw and simple and awaiting branding by SEA Design.

146\
Collaborating
with
Clients

Bowling Together
by Adam Hart

If we were honest, we would admit that normal business relationships are generally formal and constrained. It is rare for the parties in a commercial venture to share a vision, culture or set of values which can introduce subtle yet significant qualities into the work in hand. Nor do conventional relations provide the framework for both parties to go the extra mile to achieve excellence. Such normal business relationships are not really engaged in achieving a common goal wider than a fair payment in exchange for specific services.

The extra ingredients that turn a business relationship into true collaboration can be illustrated by the joint working of Hackney Co-operative Developments (HCD) and Hawkins\Brown. It is a complex story, but one which is worth telling; it shows the degree of commitment required to achieve truly collaborative architecture. Hackney Co-operative Developments is a local-community economic development organisation constituted in 1982 with a membership open for all those who subscribe to its co-operative goals and values, to provide workspace to nurture and support emerging local businesses.

From 1994 HCD and Hawkins\Brown have collaborated on a series of building projects in London's North-East district of Dalston that have included the rehabilitation and extension of a Victorian street terrace (Bradbury Street Community Workspace), a series of prefabricated market pods (Gillett Street), a fluorescent cultural venue (the Dalston Culture House) and a new town square (Gillett Square). Together these works amount to a form of incremental, 'bottom-up' development informed by a collective vision (rather than just a masterplan) for this special part of the London Borough of Hackney.

Popular representations of this area's economy tend to paint a negative picture, referring to its piles of rubbish, poverty, crime, drug dealers, prostitution, street people, vagrants, squatters and alcoholics. But in its totality the real picture, and Dalston's possible future, is very different. Here we have nearly every kind of food in the shops and restaurants and take-aways: Indian, Italian, Bangladeshi, Pakistani, Russian, Anatolian, Turkish, Kurdish, Greek, African, Caribbean, and South-East Asian, Chinese. The area is the UK home of reggae and hip-hop, reputedly it has more nightclubs than the West End, and more artists than anywhere else in Europe. It is home to the Rio Cinema and the Arcola Street Theatre, which together provide a rich variety of mainstream and arthouse productions, it is also home to the Centerprise and Stoke Newington bookshops, the Vortex Jazz Club, and a whole number of galleries. It redefines contemporary understandings of diversity.

Daily shopping has been sustained for many years by the huge Ridley Road Market where cheap food from all around the world is mixed with music, clothes and DVDs. Many thousands of people pour into the area every day to shop in the market. Across the High Street from Ridley Road, is the Bradbury Street area which was first brought back into use from almost complete dereliction by HCD in 1982. Until recently this area has been marginal, providing car parking and some early market leads – such as whole foods, complementary medicines and bicycle repair services.

By the mid 1980s Bradbury Street had become a lively place for small co-operative businesses and voluntary organisations. HCD's surveys found popular support for the area to become pedestrianised and for a market. In 1994 HCD selected Hawkins\Brown to work on its European (the Objective 2 Regional Development Fund, ERDF) and Central Government (Single Regeneration Budget, SRB) bids to redevelop the Bradbury Street premises on a long-term basis, as the first phase of an area regeneration programme that continues to this day.

The choice of Hawkins\Brown was based on their modern design skills, their experience of working in the community sector, and the fact that they lived locally in Hackney. The Bradbury Street regeneration drew much acclaim from the architectural world and stands out as one of the most prominent legacies of these funding programmes. But it was the beginning of a story as much as an ending.

In 1999, HCD's second project with Hawkins\Brown was to build ten market pods along the south side of the car park, helping develop the idea of a new town square in Gillett Street (in 1998 the London Borough of Hackney [LBH] Regeneration Committee

designated the car park as a future town square), and coming to national prominence as the winner of the RIBA small building award in 1999 and of the Design Week Award for 2000. HCD's next move was to formulate a project to redevelop the adjacent derelict factory at 11 Gillett Street to create the Dalston Culture House. The lead occupant and early partner in this project became the world-famous Vortex Jazz Club.

The arrival of the Vortex Jazz Club in the Dalston Culture House has helped to trigger a UK-wide wave of interest in cutting-edge jazz and world music amongst a new audience. It also attracted attention to the Hackney area. In 2000 these developments aroused the interest of developers MacDonald Egan, who had recently purchased the decaying Stamford Works premises occupying the north side of Gillett Street. They appointed Hawkins\Brown to develop a series of housing schemes, the first phase of which was completed in 2006. This helped set the scene for the delivery of the long-envisaged public space to replace the car park and the formation of the Gillett Square Partnership as the development agency.

As the success of the area grew, so the number of project partners grew and the collaboration became more complex. In its final form the Partnership included HCD, Groundwork East London, LBH Planning, Leisure and Property Directorates, MacDonald Egan and Hawkins\Brown. The architects were not simply passive designers in this process. They first proposed and then helped to create the Partnership, undertook the feasibility work and coordinated the meetings, funding applications and contracted work. In 2003 this partnership expanded to include the Vortex and, through the adoption by the Greater London Authority (GLA) of Gillett Square as one of Mayor Livingstone's new urban spaces for London, representatives of the GLA's Architecture and Urbanism Unit (AAUU).

There can be no more complex collaboration detailed in this book than this one. The Partnership won further capital funding and worked up a design brief for tender and construction through the Borough of Hackney. The spectacular launch of the Square in November 2006 was organised through the Gillett Square Partnership, the managing and accountable body being HCD, principally involving the Vortex Jazz Club, the East London Design Show and the LBH Culture Department. The event will be remembered by many as one of London's most inspiring and engaging public events in 2006, and showed off the Square as an immense new community asset.

But to sustain such a complex process, there needs to be more than professional respect between architect and client. It is no exaggeration to say that our form of collaboration resonates with the historic forms of the master builder and landed entrepreneur. These have gradually moved apart over the past 500 years and led to the emergence of the architect, client and builder as distinct professions, whose relationships are governed by numerous contractual rules. However inevitable and useful this differentiation may be, there are good reasons to argue that this development has left something very important out of the process needed to create really outstanding built environments.

These missing elements – and I think our collaborative work with Hawkins\Brown, and particularly Russell Brown, has touched upon them over the past 15 years – is the subject of this essay. My thesis is that these crucial elements are not in fundamental contradiction to the modern, complex forms of role differentiation. Rather these neglected aspects are in fact the keys to the future that can rescue us from current dystopian, 'Junk City' developments, and all the appalling dross of late capitalism and its prima-donna, celebrity architects.

We are not talking here about an 'over-cosy' or corrupt relationship for selfish aims between the client developer and architect, but rather what happens when architect and client developer are aligned with and working within a set of public values in which the continuum of culture and community is as important as short-term money or fame. Collaboration, especially when there is a strong and inspiring vision at play (in the context of opposition from all quarters), can mean that the work performed goes far beyond the normal value for money/labour inputs. Except in jest it would be a mistake to call this a conspiracy. And why should this sense of purpose not be found more often than it is? For two reasons:

- There is a general lack of holism in production and service delivery caused by growing specialisation and professionalisation in an increasingly complex, high-technology society.
- There is also a specific lack of input from the end-users in design and management processes brought about by the erosion of local democracy and community ownership.

These issues have become central themes in many progressive regeneration policy-making documents of the last two decades. Much admirable vision and rhetoric from Central Government level have contained strategic promptings to bring these missing

elements back into the equation. But there have been few actual enactments of this vision on the ground.

This is what makes HCD's work in Dalston with Hawkins\Brown so exceptional. The quality of the outcome suggests that this is indeed a better way of doing things. As with all path-finding journeys there are battles that we fought and crises that we had to face that may not confront those who follow this route, with the benefit of HCD's experience. And others may not share the same luck that HCD experienced from time to time, as when, for instance, the long-nurtured proposals for Gillett Square chimed with Mayor Livingstone's announcement in 2003 of his 100 New Spaces for Londoners programme.

Visitors to Gillett Square in Dalston, and its many architectural students, quickly recognise that there is something special about this place, something right. There is something more in the whole here than the quality of the specific design elements, its curtilage buildings and the surface of the square itself, the judicious mix of old and new or the scale and layering. Something more than the growing number of arts, community and market events in the square, or the gathering momentum of often fascinating spontaneous uses, by all ages of a diverse population.

The specialness of Gillett Square relates to the underlying set of social and practical relationships of production that have brought about the making of this space. The extent to which the relations of production of the built environment permeate the experience of that environment is largely unaddressed outside the field of social anthropology. Urban sociologists, such as Manuel Castells, have for long proposed that when we look at an urban landscape what we experience is not so much a set of three-dimensional space-time objects, but rather a reading, or at least a sensing, of the social, legal and economic process that it represents.

These relationships determine our perceptions and appear to both seep into, and ooze out of, the material objects that constitute the 'site'. They are something akin to its DNA, its genetic structure; they determine the site's manifestation and pervade the particular 'sense of place'. In other words these relationships reflect a collective consciousness behind the act of creation, and, as one of Jack Kerouac's rules of poetics goes, "if the mind is shapely the art is shapely". So how are these relationships defined in this case? In our work with Hawkins\ Brown they can be grouped into personal, parochial and public categories:

The first of these lies in the personal/cultural domain. After the formal interview process to select suitable community architects, Russell Brown and I (as the Executive Director of HCD) discovered two important personal things that we have in common, along with many of our friends and partners. We are both experienced builders (I have the rare distinction of both Oxbridge and Dudley Skill Centre certifications), and architecture and music is a central part of our lives. As builders we share a passion to get things made. In music we think that improvisation really counts. As Duke Ellington, for whom music was his mistress, said "if it ain't got that swing it don't mean a thing!"

These overlaps (and others such as sharing the same local pub, The Prince George) have set the scene for a shared appreciation of architecture's craft and its aesthetics, in which the structural basis and concepts of music can act as an illuminating linguistic reference point. Both the organisations have a deeply rooted involvement and respect for the charitable and voluntary sector in East London. This reflects a shared attitude to parochial and professional matters. We have the same values of social morality. This underpins an enthusiastic vision of this sector's great potential when coupled to entrepreneurial professionalism. These intersections have led us to take calculated risks together and invest time and energy in worthwhile but daunting projects in the neighbourhood.

And of course we must work together with other public bodies and institutions. Most of our work together has involved asset transfer and capital grant projects from the European, national and local public sector. As such our client/architect brief goes well beyond dealing with planning, design and construction issues and covers many other things such as working together on the project's business plan, the assembly of a financial package, gaining the support and confidence of local politicians, dealing with risk-averse local authority legal departments, grant funders' tortuous monitoring, claim and procurement procedures, as well as consultations and confrontations with elements in the local community that may be at various times enthusiastic and willing supporters, fierce opponents or wily exploiters of the project.

It is within these domains of shared experience, skill and vision that collaboration takes place. In our case there are many examples that span the whole gamut of research, planning, development and construction, operations that start with feasibility studies and run all the way through to end usage, marketing, and appraisal. A few instances illustrate this point.

Many of the key design concepts for the Bradbury Street area regeneration emerged from our conversations, such as

- The introduction of deck entries on the upper floors of the terrace to create passive surveillance for the future public square. (1995)
- The idea for flexible market pods came from our shared experience of Italian and Latin American newsstands. (1999)
- The idea to provide Dalston Culture House with a celebratory, luminous frontage. (2003)
- The concept of Gillett Square as a space that would function as a multipurpose outdoor theatre. (2003)

When HCD first started on the rehabilitation of Bradbury Street, they had to convince the local authority that they had a viable regeneration scheme. Without Hawkins\Brown's assistance with the ERDF and SRB bids and the practice's 'blue chip' credentials the refurbishment appraisals would have carried no weight against the demolition and redevelopment scheme promoted by a local housing association. In the end, the alternative scheme survived the scrutiny of several highly paid regeneration consultancies, and won the day. The scheme was not only judged viable, but more than this it was perceived as serving the needs of economically and socially excluded groups. It attracted public funding offers from outside Hackney that the local authority could not be seen to be turning away.

The collaboration worked quickly when unexpected problems arose. In 1996 several problem tenants threatened to halt building works in Bradbury Street and cut off our funding. Hawkins\Brown joined HCD in intensive consultations with these tenants. They also presented to emergency sessions with the funding bodies to steady their nerves. They provided supporting evidence that helped sway the legal arguments in our favour. In 2003 the local authority announced, on the eve of the sale of the site for the Dalston Culture House, that they no longer owned it on account of an 'adverse possession' order. Hawkins\Brown simply moved the scheme 6 metres to the east and negotiated a revised planning consent. The subsequent release of additional space for the Culture House then generated a second phase of works in 2006. In this way the collaboration turned what could have been complete disaster into a net gain for the neighbourhood.

Our decision to work closely with local partners was fundamental as well; with a view towards extending our own attitude to collaboration to others, for better or worse, in 2001 we brought together all the key actors and owners in and around the Gillett Street car park under the heading of the Gillett Square Partnership. This successful partnership, engaging all three sectors (the private, voluntary and public) on an equal footing, is now being widely studied as a model for the devolved governance and community ownership of public space.

Such seemingly natural collaboration appears to have been born out of a special set of circumstances, cultural affinities and motivation. Clearly we embarked upon this venture with an almost innate sense of its social worth and with a determination to do whatever was necessary to get things done. In retrospect, the benefits which our departure from the usual ways of working together and our challenges to conventional regeneration practices have brought are convincing enough for us – and others – to continue along the same road.

Shifting the norm away from formal business relationships, which tend to give centre place to the employer/employee, customer/provider and consumer/producer forms of relationship, and focusing instead on the notion of a conjoined, affective and empathetic working relationship, has allowed us to nurture more successfully the goal of holistic community economic development – a space where 'bottom-up' meets 'top-down' and joined-up thinking and delivery is governed by the underview as much as by the overview.

The unique collaboration between Hawkins\Brown and HCD has produced a special result that pervades the experience of this site and acts as a major impetus for Dalston's ongoing regeneration. But it may also signal that there remains an occasional possibility, even under advanced capitalism, to subvert the nightmare of coldly rational corporate machinations described by the famous sociologist Max Weber in his studies of the dynamics of rationality and bureaucracy in the industrial world. It may offer a model in which lore can tame law and the spirit of community can have some real and stable meaning. Because of such pioneering work we have arrived at the stage where such a way might gain more permanent expression in new institutional forms, such as a Neighbourhood Development Trust, or a new form of Parish Council for the inner city.

Opposite The Culture House, Hackney, London.

Student Enterprise Building, Coventry University

Hawkins\Brown won this project because the Vice Chancellor saw them as committed to talking and listening to the students who will use the new Student Enterprise Building. As the majority of students at Coventry University live at home and commute into the city centre each day, they need a place to eat, complete their work, meet together or just sit down out of the rain. The new building will be the geographical, urban and cultural heart of the campus that everyone passes through on their way to and from lectures. It will be the place to meet and make connections, the University's new 'living room'.

The project has developed a deliberately provocative and startling image that is very different from the institutional 1960s blocks of the rest of Coventry city centre. The imagery, the layouts and the programme have been developed in a continuous dialogue with students and the University officers who will work together to make the new building a success.

Starting with visits to student centres around the country, observing the management, listening to the users' needs and aspirations, analysing issues in the existing buildings, testing solutions and building models, the architects developed a design that was supported by different stakeholders.

The Student Enterprise Building covers 8,500 square metres over two floors, so that all spaces in the building are closely related to the busiest walking routes across the campus. The less public areas of the building rise to four storeys where it faces the Cathedral and onto Jordan Well. The roof plane protected by these 'bookends' forms a vast roof terrace that will significantly increase the amount of open, green space in this urban campus.

The building 'twists and turns' across the site, deliberately forming new external spaces through the campus with active edges, making new connections to building entrances and popular routes outside the site. The building is as transparent as possible so that the exciting activities inside attract students; it is to be perceived as 'anti-institutional', safe and accessible.

The majority of the building's internal spaces are available for 'social learning' where students can work together in groups, supported by cutting-edge information technology, presentation and conferencing facilities. The traditional Student Union facilities of bars and venues are included but not allowed to dominate the management or feel of the building.

The University is seeking a building that is informal and welcoming to young people, placed somewhere between the academic and business worlds. In the long term there will be a synergy with the proposed adjacent New Ways of Working Building, which is to attract inward investment through partnerships with local businesses and will act as a laboratory for new working practices.

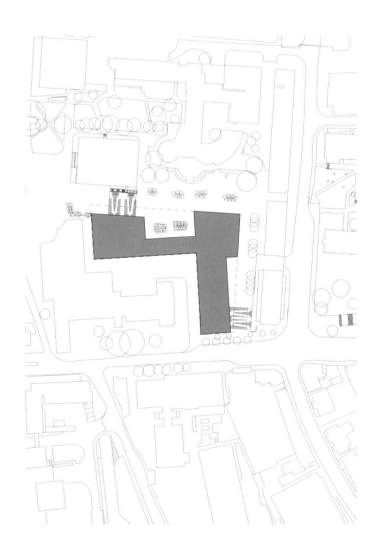

Above Site plan (1:2500).

Opposite The entrance courtyard offers protected amenity space for students.

Above A 1:75 model was used to test furniture layouts and internal spaces in the reception and informal learning areas.

Below Large items of bespoke furniture have been designed by Hawkins\Brown to punctuate spaces and provide intimate study and social areas.

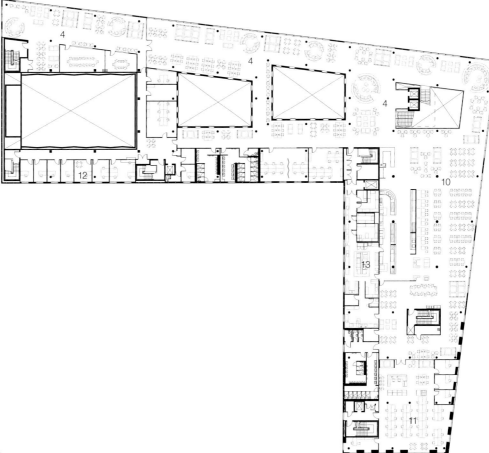

First floor plan (1:750).

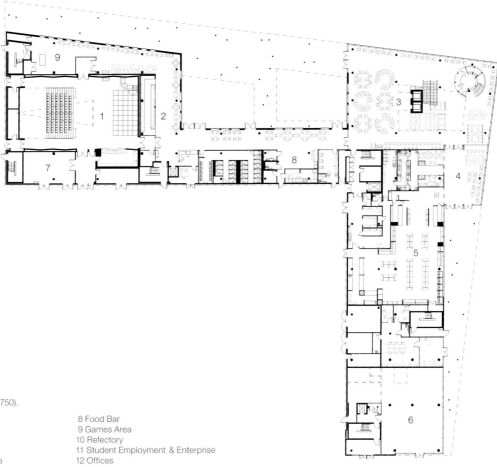

Ground floor plan (1:750).

1 Event Space
2 Bar
3 Reception
4 Informal Learning
5 Convenience Store
6 Bookshop
7 Store

8 Food Bar
9 Games Area
10 Refectory
11 Student Employment & Enterprise
12 Offices
13 Kitchen

Above Monochrome fritted bands
wrap the glazed façade, suggesting
dynamic movement.

Opposite The building will be utilised
as much at night as in the daytime;
it includes a much needed night club
and music venue for Coventry.

The Terrace,
Southwark, London

Financing a speculative commercial development like More London is a tricky undertaking even in the case of a prime location like this. For Liam Bond, however, this was perhaps the least of his difficulties. He is the Development Director for More London and, effectively, landlord to the Mayor. Hawkins\Brown first came into contact with him in 2000 when they came second in the competition to design the Unicorn Children's Theatre, which is situated at the very edge of Norman Foster's masterplan.

The terrace of buildings in Tooley Street, behind the new City Hall, not only sits within the masterplan, but also within the North Bermondsey Conservation Area. Liam Bond's idea for the Terrace was for it to act as a bridge: a transition zone – within the retained building project – between the emerging condition of More London and the area's more traditional residential scale. Hawkins\Brown were invited to work closely with Bond to liberate as much floor space as possible. The architects developed a façade strategy, determining that it would be best to remove and replace two old buildings rather than create a pastiche 'infill' design. Tooley Street would be a hybrid of old and new that would reflect this unique area.

In order to maximise the usable space, Hawkins\Brown determined that the party walls could be opened up and, by being imaginative with floor levels, the whole basement space could be brought into active use. Together with Liam Bond, they considered how the building could be used, either by a series of different tenants or just one. Possible users included public bodies, charities or a housing association, while the architects also considered the space as a public library in the model of the Idea Stores. All of these options were seriously thought through and tested, which was a very different conversation than the client's other discussions, such as convincing Ernst & Young, one of the world's largest accounting firms, to become tenants in the huge, institutional More London office buildings.

The completed Tooley Terrace redevelopment has recently been leased by Red Bull, who have taken the whole site as their headquarters. They have worked closely with the original intent of the design, creating an interior that reflects the concept of the balloon within a teacup, whereby the 'host' building thoughtfully supports its newly reinvigorated interior life.

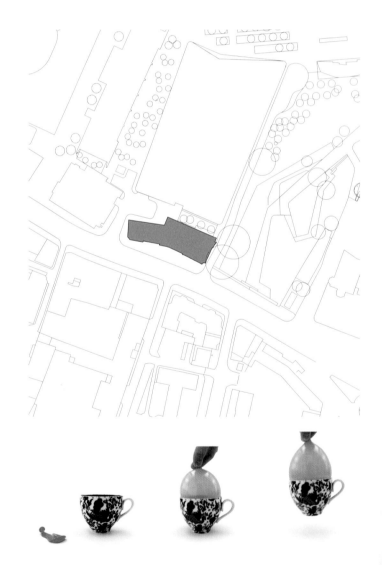

Above Site plan (1:2000).

Below Concept: the teacup as host to the new balloon intervention, a metaphor for the existing terrace and its new addition.

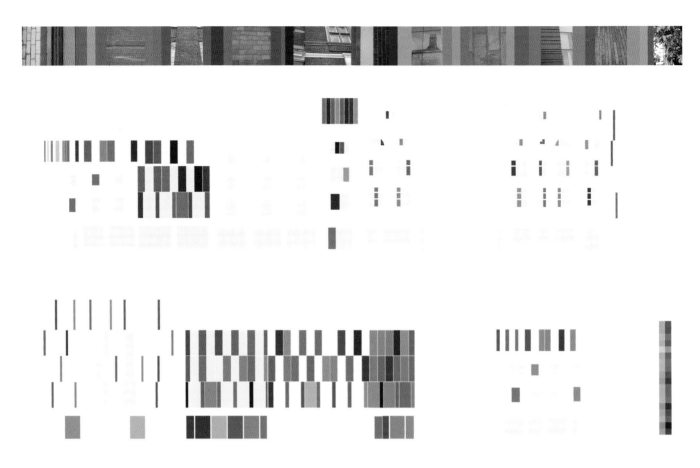

Above Sampling the local context to develop a sympathetic colour palette.

Below The impact of coloured glazing on the interior.

Opposite above The new extension nestles amongst the existing buildings

and creates large open-plan spaces behind a more sympathetic façade.

Opposite below At night the orange and brown glass glows brightly announcing the building to passers-by on Tooley Street.

Parliament Square, Westminster, London

To say that the Parliament Square project had a complex and powerful client body would be something of an understatement. The Steering Group featured representatives from the Greater London Authority, Westminster City Council, the Royal Parks, Transport for London, Metropolitan Police, English Heritage, Westminster Abbey, Parliamentary Estates, Her Majesty's Court Service, Cabinet Office and Design for London. Not only were Hawkins\Brown dealing directly with Britain's legislature, through the Parliamentary Estates, but also its executive, in the shape of the Cabinet Office. They were also consulting with the Church of England at the highest level, the Crown, and the top tier of the judiciary, the Supreme Court. All of these institutions had a stake in Parliament Square.

Precisely because of the power of these stakeholders and the web of vested interests between them, every major attempt to improve this space since it was turned into a traffic island by the Ministry of Transport in the 1940s has failed. The consequences which this clumsy democratic process entails for one of the UK's major landmarks are depressing. The narrow pavements around the Mother of all Parliaments are thronged with tens of thousands of people each day, but only a few are actually permitted onto the square outside, and only if they are willing to dare the traffic on this clockwise gyratory as it rushes between the City and Victoria. It is an aberration which surely needs to be addressed. And yet the proposal drawn up by the team under the aegis of the Parliament Square Governance Group, which included Hawkins\Brown as lead architects, was quietly shelved in 2008 along with a number of other public space projects in the City.

The delay is deplorable all the more so because the plan is poised perfectly between symbolism and practicalities. To permit increased usage, Hawkins\Brown realised they would have to elect for hard landscaping. Eschewing the corporate taste for Chinese granite, the square's design team opted instead for traditional paving techniques, even going so far as to look at sourcing separate stones from different parts of the country. They also looked at introducing native species of trees to the planted section of the square. The political significance of the project was never lost: "We wanted to reflect this notion of democracy", says Roger Hawkins. As well as retaining the existing statuary, the design also included plans for a round table, or a rather a table abstracted into a sunken circular form which gave vantage points of Big Ben and Westminster Abbey.

Above The proposed square would replace a busy traffic island with a major new public space for London.

Opposite Siteplan (1:1500).

The existing square is largely inaccessible and pedestrians are forced to move around the square through a series of pedestrian crossings.

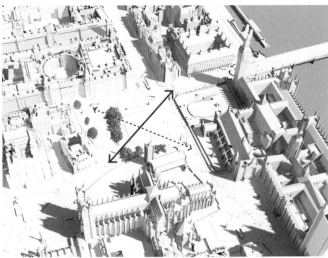

New crossings and desire lines: by introducing a series of pedestrian crossings the pedestrians' natural desire lines can be accommodated.

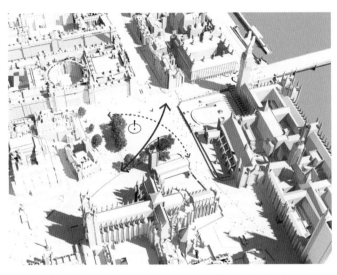

Curved pedestrian routes create a new understanding of the relationships between the new square and the historic assets around it. Two new spaces are created between these main routes.

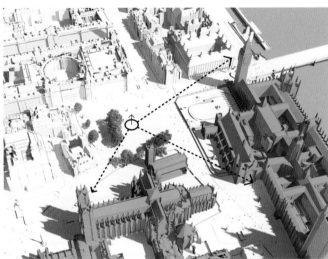

The Round Table offers improved views of Big Ben and other world heritage sites whilst existing trees and sculptures continue to provide shelter and interest.

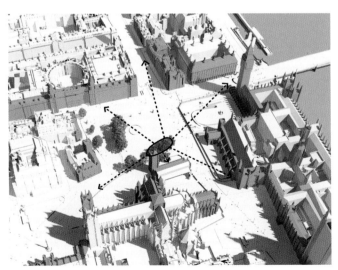

The Copse, a thicket of trees, offers a more tranquil space with an alternative view to other traditional surrounding buildings.

The new square is paved in a Fibonacci rose pattern reflecting the new lines of focus. The paving stones diminish in size and vary in material to reflect the new hierarchy.

Above The proposed new Parliament   Below The square as it is now.
Square.

New Faculty of Business and Law, Kingston University, London

The real impact of the Further and Higher Education Acts 1992 is only now being felt. This act enabled thirty-five polytechnics to become universities. It also created national funding bodies, removed colleges of further education from local government control and created a funding structure tied to performance assessment. The slow drip-feed of capital funding is now beginning to make its mark. Kingston University, which was established as Kingston Technical Institute in 1899, and later became known as Kingston Polytechnic, is a classic example of this process. Its four dispersed campuses have been developed in an ad-hoc fashion, responding to annual injections of limited funding, and now they are in substantial need of revitalisation and rationalisation.

An accommodation study and masterplanning exercise was undertaken by Hawkins\Brown in 2008. This took into account the principles identified within the University's Campus Development Plans, but went into more architectural detail on the Kingston Hill and Penrhyn Road sites. At Kingston Hill, a new learning resources centre had been designed by John McAslan, and now the focus is on a new £30 million teaching building which will complete the second side of the 'town square' envisaged in Hawkins\Brown's plans for this campus.

The new Faculty of Business and Law will occupy the site of Rennie Hall, a run-down hall of residence from the 1950s. Design work began in June 2008 in parallel with the masterplanning. Planning consent was given for a tightly planned courtyard-style building constructed of traditional materials. The design is distinctly modernist but is sympathetic to the Campus's woodland setting and its status as a Conservation Area. The new building is set into a steeply sloping site, so that it links the campus on three different levels. Although a relatively discreet project, it will transform walking routes across the campus by providing clear links between the major levels of the campus and establishing a new destination with its central 'social learning' and café space.

Each elevation has a different character determined by the context, activities and open space on that side. The building is entered on all four sides, so the landscape is activated by the users. Students are led quickly into what Russell Brown calls the 'donut', a dramatic circulation space at the building's core so that the new Faculty of Business and Law can be both a thoroughfare and an easily accessible teaching facility.

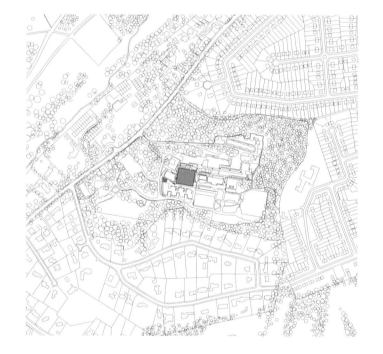

Above Site plan (1:10000).

Opposite above The top-lit internal courtyard will be used for informal learning.

Opposite below A recessed top floor provides uninterrupted views across the campus.

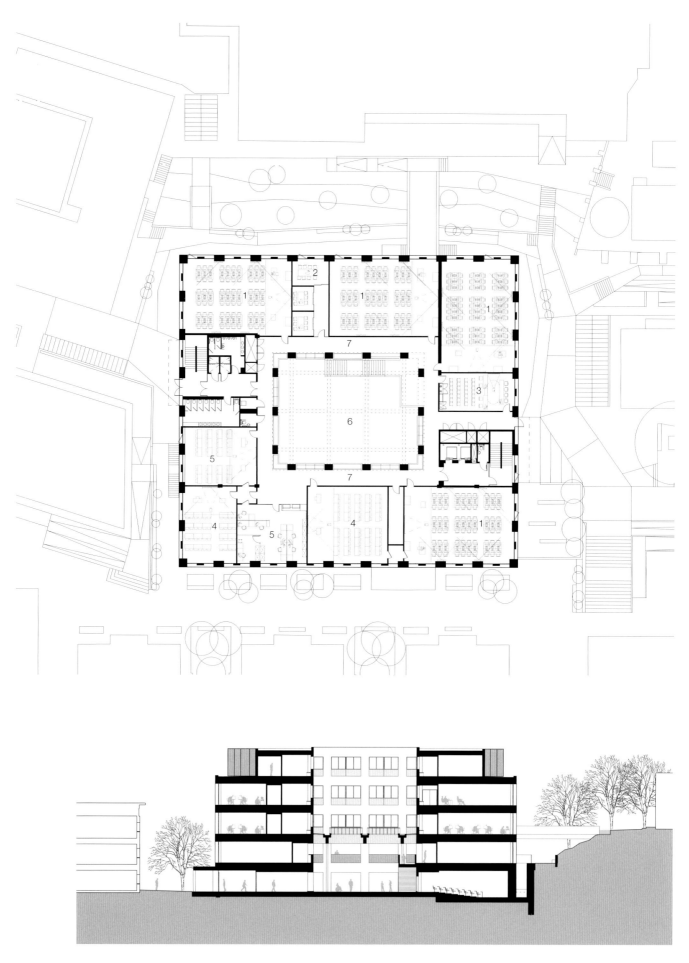

Above Second floor plan and section (1:500).

1 60 Seat Computer Room
2 Meeting Rooms
3 Moot Court Room
4 Classroom

5 Technical Support Office
6 Informal Learning Space (below)
7 Built-in banquette seating & laptop bars.

Opposite Detail (1:80).

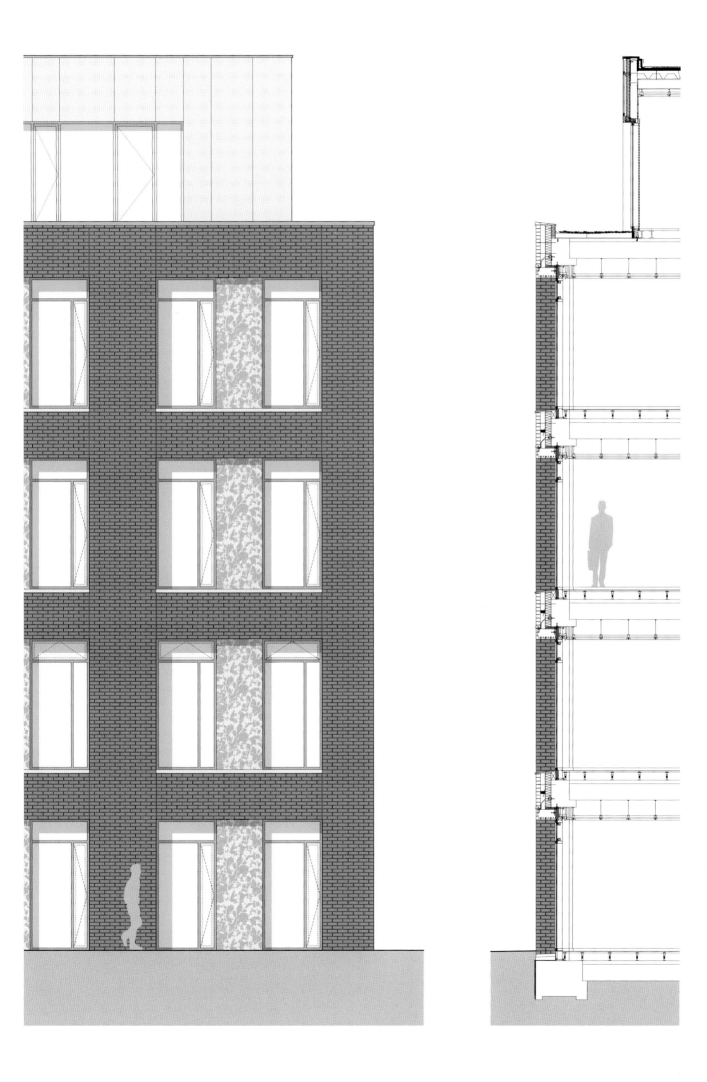

New Biochemistry, University of Oxford

Working for Oxford University on an extended basis, Hawkins\ Brown have learned that collaborating with a complex client – including the University's executive body, the Estates Department and the academic users – can actually augment the design process for a building rather than deflect or confuse it. At Oxford, the Director of Estates and Head of Projects have experience as commercial developers who understand the lives of buildings from inception to construction and from use to re-use. For the New Biochemistry building, there was an extensive group of users, who despite some early reticence, came to treat the architect team as a fellow expert who could dramatically improve the environment in which they carry out their research.

One of the main aims of the new building was to attract the very best researchers in a highly competitive, worldwide market. As Denis O'Driscoll, the Associate Head of Biochemistry points out, they wanted to create a spectacular building that students and researchers would want to come and work in, not just because it is in Oxford, but because it is a 'happening building'. They wanted a space that promotes and facilitates scientific research, and that would consolidate the operations of the Department, which previously were scattered among seven different buildings. This new 12,000-square-metre structure brought together more than 300 scientists and their highly specialist equipment into a single unifying building.

In discussion with Oxford's planners the architects saw the surrounding buildings in the Science Area as having a mostly vertical emphasis. This is in contrast to the eminently horizontal forms of modernist strip windows and expressed floor plates. The four-storey glass fins that make up the elevations of the new building create a strong vertical rhythm across an extensive elevation to Hinchelwood Road. The colours of the fins reflect the tones of the building materials of Oxford: orange, yellow and ochre ironstone, purple and red-blue bricks. The colour and transparency of the fins create elevations that change throughout the day and with the weather, casting bands of coloured light into the laboratory floors or out onto the surrounding streets. Through the complex design of the elevations the building manages to be both open to the world around it and contribute to it.

Inside, the building's layout deliberately challenges the academic convention of scientists working on independent projects in

Above The main entrance from the new courtyard is marked by Nicky Hirst's 'Rorschach' artwork.

Opposite Hawkins\Brown will have a major influence on central Oxford through a number of projects.

1 New Biochemistry Phase 1
2 New Department of Physics
3 Department of Engineering, Science, Thom Building
4 Relocated Jericho Health Centre
5 Queen Elizabeth House
6 New Biochemistry Phase 2
7 Department of Physiology, Anatomy & Genetics
8 Doctoral Training Centre
9 Tinsley Building Refurbishment

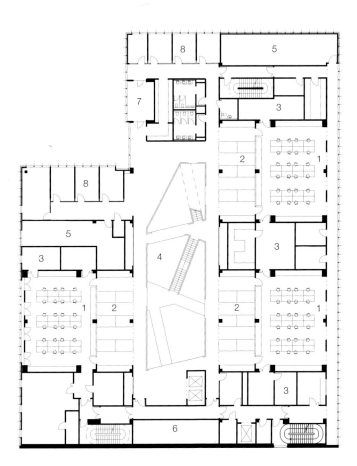

Second floor plan (1:500).

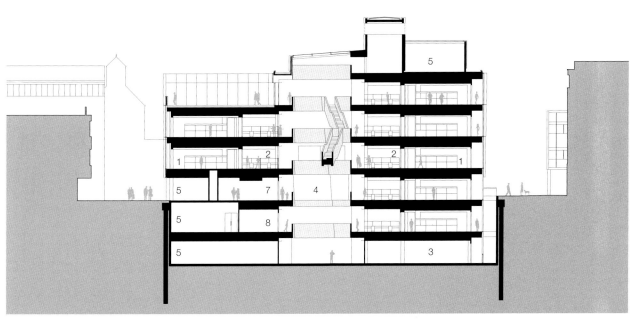

Section (1:500).

Opposite A view of the central atrium
space, with the stairs linking the
different write-up spaces and artwork
by Nicky Hirst and Annie Cattrell.

1 Main Laboratory
2 Write-up Spaces
3 Support/Specialist Laboratory
4 Atrium

5 Plant
6 Ancilliary Space
7 Seminar/ Meeting Room
8 Offices

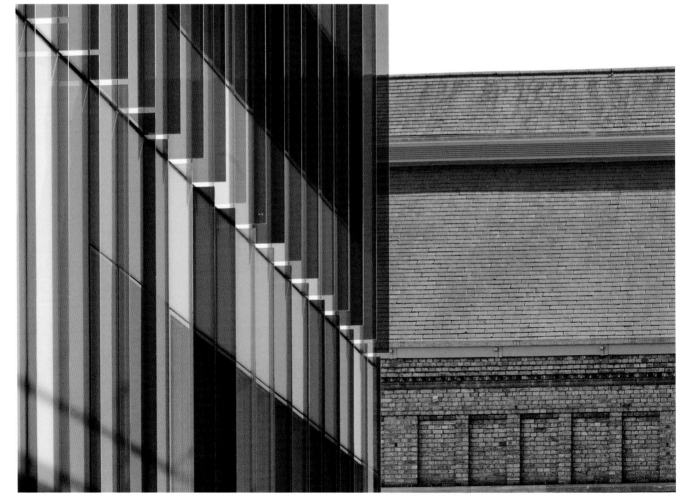

181

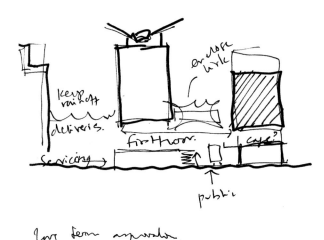

long term aspiration.

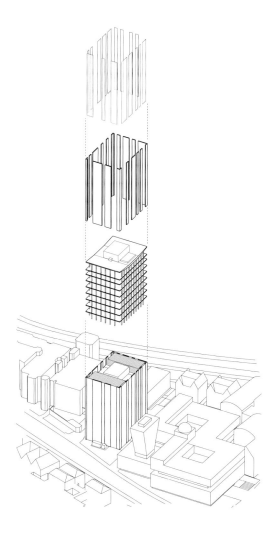

secluded laboratories. The design's key principle was to bring people together in a single space, encouraging collaboration through visual connection and chance meetings. The staircases that criss-cross from floor to floor have become the central arteries of the building, visually representing these links and literally encouraging dynamic movement between different research groups. Informal meeting spaces are scattered through the six levels. Open-plan write-up areas and glass-fronted offices surrounding the atrium maintain this transparency and promote a sense of community. This central space is home to art work as well as a grand piano.

Curated by Morag Morrison and artist Nicky Hirst, the specially commissioned pieces explore the relationship between art and science. Working closely with Hawkins\Brown and research professors to create integrated pieces, Hirst herself designed the glass façade around the entrance and a piece called *Portal* in the café.

The same planning authorities that encourage the vertical orientation of the new buildings have also determined that buildings must not be too tall, so no new structure in Oxford can be higher than the Carfax Tower. As the University wanted to maximise the accommodation on site, it was necessary to excavate two basement levels, but the atrium brings daylight down to the lower floor so that internally it feels like six linked floors. Already a massive project, the second phase will bring the accommodation capacity up to 800 scientists sharing this communal space.

As part of the development study for the New Biochemistry building, Hawkins\Brown were asked by the University to masterplan the core of the Science Area. This involved looking at creating new pedestrian-friendly spaces, resolving servicing and parking, and establishing the mass and forms for new science buildings. The architects recently completed a sensitive upgrade to Queen Elizabeth House in place of an undistinguished 1930s addition and have won the competition for a new Centre for Theoretical and Experimental Physics. This will be a further step in the execution of their masterplan for the Science Area. The fruitful and successful co-operation between Oxford University and Hawkins\Brown continues.

Opposite above New Biochemistry - The density of the fins and the colour changes as the observer moves around the building.

Opposite below The vertical emphasis of the glass fins and the choice of colours reflect the context around the building.

Above Concept sketch by Russell Brown for refurbishing the Thom Building.

Below Concept diagram by Russell Brown for re-cladding the structure.

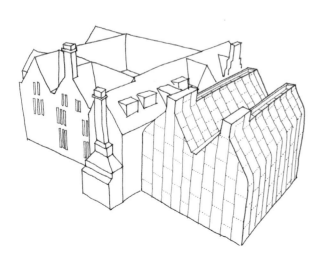

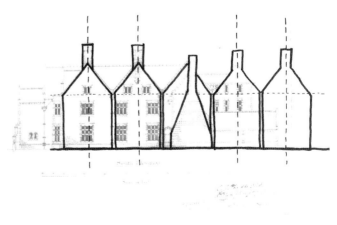

Opposite Competition-winning proposal for the Theoretical and Experimental Physics Building at the University of Oxford.

Above The forms and materials of Queen Elizabeth House echo the forms of the listed building that it extends.

Gillett Square, Hackney, London

The extension of the East London Line into Dalston, as part of the newly established London Overground network, is one of the main reasons why this long-neglected area of London is experiencing a boom in development. The close proximity of a dizzying range of ethnic restaurants, bars and clubs contributes to this newfound attraction. As a result, Kingsland Road is one of the most vibrant and multi-cultural streets in the capital. However, it is the contribution of Adam Hart, executive director of Hackney Co-operative Developments (HCD), that has turned this unlikely London village from development hotspot into a truly engaging and attractive place. It is his leadership and the designs of Hawkins\Brown that have made this a part of London where you would want to live rather than just visit or invest.

Hart joined HCD in 1992, having worked as a bricklayer, a social researcher and for a number of social enterprises around London. In 1993, HCD first commissioned the sketches of a new town square in Gillett Street. It took until 1998, after several local public consultations, for Hackney Council's Regeneration Committee to agree to designate the Gillett Street car park as the future town square for Dalston. Anyone who went to the official opening of Gillett Square would have thought that the Council's support for the square had been long-standing. It took a further ten years to raise the funds and organise the work.

Adam Hart's relationship with Hawkins\Brown began when they came up with a proposal to stop the demolition of Bradbury Street, which still forms the south side of the Square. Hart's vision for the retained Victorian terrace was for small incubator studio units above workshops, linked together by a new training and administrative centre. Hawkins\Brown responded with a circular tower building that was the first sign of regeneration in the area.

Just as HCD's ethos is to foster business development from small beginnings, so their approach has always been to make the square work incrementally. In 1999 HCD and Hawkins\Brown built ten prefabricated market kiosks along the south side of the car park. These minute kiosks act as the affordable beginnings for local businesses and give a unique activity to Gillett Square.

Russell Brown and Adam Hart are friends, and they are both interested in the humane, socially progressive development of this tiny corner of London. Together they developed a project to replace the derelict factory premises in Gillett Street with the Culture House. This was completed in February 2005 with the arrival of the Vortex Jazz Club. In parallel, the work around Gillett Square engaged the interest of developers MacDonald Egan, who had recently purchased the decaying Stamford Works premises occupying the north side of Gillett Street. Hawkins\Brown developed a mixed-use scheme for this site, including a new public library for the area. The first phase was completed at the same time as the Culture House.

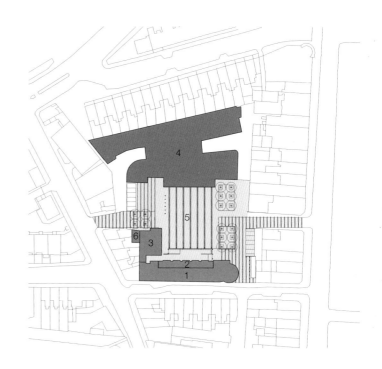

Above Gillett Square site plan.
1 Community workshops
2 Market stalls
3 The Culture House
4 Stamford Works
5 Gillett Square
6 No 1+2 Gillett Square

Opposite The Culture House and Gillett Square.

By 2001, the momentum had picked up for the Square project to such an extent that the Gillett Square Partnership was formed, effectively a development agency for Gillett Square. In 2003 Gillett Square was adopted as one of Mayor Livingstone's new urban spaces for London, which led to the involvement of the Architecture and Urbanism Unit of the Greater London Authority in the Gillett Square Partnership. The Partnership brought together HCD, Hawkins\Brown as architects, enablers and urbanists, the Borough of Hackney as landowners and development control/planners, Groundwork East and MacDonald Egan.

This remains a unique alliance of the public, private and voluntary sector and a pioneering model for the development and management of public space. It was always critical to the project that the public space, owned by the London Borough of Hackney, remained in public ownership and control.

When Gillett Square opened at Christmas 2007, the full story behind its creation, which spans 15 years of incremental development of the Bradbury and Gillett Street area of Dalston, was perhaps lost. Its incredible success is testament to the series of young architects from Hawkins\Brown – Vicky Emmet, Andy Puncher and Beth Kay – who all have been mentored by this unique client and the studio through these complex projects. Those who were involved closely, such as Russell Brown, know that the success story of the square crucially relied on Hart's "principles of consulting local businesses and working slowly with the local authority for better or worse to produce organic growth".

Above The creation of the new square reveals the secret life of the buildings along Kingsland High Road.

Below The party wall of the old building is retained within the new Culture House.

Opposite above Polycarbonate cladding transforms into an illuminated sign at night.

Opposite below View of the Culture House, Gillett Square.

189\
Project Information

020
Parkhill

Location	Sheffield, UK
Client	Urban Splash
Value	£120m
Date	Completion 2011 Phase1
	Completion 2015 all Phases
Size	130,000 m²
Contract	Construction management
Project Team	Roger Hawkins, Russell Brown, David Bickle, Antony Petrilli, Greg Moss, Seth Rutt, Daniel Burn, Iain Cochran, Seamus Lennon, Paul Westwood, Julia Roberts, Mathew Mallon, Katya Chikaher, Mark Scibberas, Mayuko Kanasugi, Teresa Telander, Mathew Mallon
Collaborators	Studio Egret West (Architects)
	Grant Associates (Landscape Architects)
	Martin Stockley Associates (Structural Engineer)
	A Models (Model Makers)
	Smoothe (CAD Visualisation)
	Squint Opera
Awards	Mail on Sunday British Homes Awards 2008
	Housing Project of the Year – Commended

026
Chichester College Redevelopment

Location	Chichester, West Sussex, UK
Client	Chichester College
Value	£100m
Date	Completion 2013
Size	42,000 m²
Contract	Two stage design and build
Project Team	Roger Hawkins, Russell Brown, David Bickle, Oliver Milton, Hazel York, Ida Hess, Jessica Billam, Anna Pamphilon, Peter Wraight, Alexander Bennett, Chloe Sharpe, Simon Parsons, Punya Sehmi, Ulrike Schwickerath.
Collaborators	Arup (Structure and Services)
	Arcadis AYH (Project Manager)
	Vogt Architects (Landscape)
	SEA Design (Graphic Designer)

026
Brinsbury Campus Redevelopment

Location	Chichester, West Sussex, UK
Client	Chichester College
Value	£30m
Date	Completion 2013
Size	25,000 m²
Contract	Two stage design and build
Project Team	Roger Hawkins, Russell Brown, David Bickle, Hazel York, Oliver Milton, Mathew Mallon, Ida Hess, Jessica Billam, Christian Matthies, Stuart Finnie, Chloe Sharpe, Mark Marshall.
Collaborators	Arup (Structure and Services)
	Davis Langdon (Cost Consultant)
	Arcadis AYH (Project Manager)
	Savills (Planning Consultant)

032\ and 114
Sevenstone New Retail Quarter

Location	Sheffield, UK
Client	Hammerson UK Plc
Value	£13m
Date	Completion 2012
Size	8,700 m²
Project Team	Roger Hawkins, Russell Brown, David Bickle, Seth Rutt, Marvin Chik, Peter van der Zwan, Petr Kalab, Lucy Dinnen.
Collaborators	Sarah Staton (Artist)
	BDP (Lead / Masterplan Architect)
	Foreign Office Architects, AHMM, O'Donnell and Tuomey, Pick Everard, ACME, Stiff & Trevillion (Block Architects)
	Gillespies (Landscape Architect)
	Arup Associates (Structural Engineers and Fire Consultant)
	WSP (Services Engineer)
	Davis Langdon (Project Manager and Quantity Surveyor)
	Pinniger & Partners (Lighting Design)

036
The Wharves

Location	Deptford, London, UK
Client	City & Provincial Properties plc
Value	£150m
Date	Planning application 2009
Size	122,000 m²
Project Team	Roger Hawkins, Russell Brown, David Bickle, Katie Tonkinson, David Lomax, Nick Rees, Alex Smith, Nick Gaskell, Campbell Metcalfe, Darryl Chen, Anna MacDougall, Jenifer O'Donnell, Michael Macleod, Nimi Attanayake, Clodagh McCallig.
Collaborators	GROSS.MAX (Landscape and Public Realm)
	CMA Planning with Savills (Planning Consultants)
	Soundings (Community Engagement)
	WSP Development and Transportation (Transport Consultant)
	Max Fordham LLP (Services Sustainability and Noise)
	Elliot Wood Partnership (Structural Engineer)
	EC Harris (Cost Consultant / Viability)
	Peter Stewart Consultancy (Townscape Consultant and Visual Impact Assessment)
	EYELEVEL (Visualiser \ Verified Views)
	Savills Research (Socio-Economic Consultant)
	Savills Development (Residential Brief)
	GVA Schatunowski Brooks (Daylight and Sunlight Consultant)
	Peter Brett Associates (Hydrology Consultant)
	CSA Environmental Planning (Ecology Consultant)
	WSP (Contamination, Air Quality and Waste)
	BRE (Wind Assessment)
	MoLAS (Archaeology)
	W H H Van Sickle Ltd (Historic Consultant)
	A Models (Model Makers)

040
Highfields Automotive & Engineering Centre

Location	Nottingham Science Park, Highfields, Nottingham, UK
Client	Castle College Nottingham / Toyota
Value	£9m
Date	Completion 2008
Size	6,600 m²
Contract	Design and build
Project Team	Roger Hawkins, Russell Brown, Jeremy Walker, Nick Gaskell, Jason Martin, Alex Smith, David Lomax, Angelique Wisse, Esther Everett
Collaborators	Studio Egret West (Masterplanners)
	Grant Associates (Landscape Architects)
	BWB Consulting (Structural Engineer)
	BDSP Partnership (Services Engineer)
	Gleeds (Quantity Surveyor)
	Antony Aspbury Associates (Planning Supervisor)
	EDCM Consulting (Utilities Engineers)
Awards	RIBA Award 2009
	RIBA LSC Further Education
	Design Excellence Award 2009

054\
Corby Cube

Location	Corby, Northamptonshire, UK
Client	Corby Borough Council
Value	£30m
Date	Completion 2010
Size	7,500 m²
Contract	Traditional, JCT2005
Project Team	Roger Hawkins, Russell Brown, Seth Rutt, Mathew Mallon, Euan Macdonald, Felix Oefelein, David Lomax, Neena Thakkar, Angelique Wisse, Chloe Sharpe, Ruth Milne, Andrew Hamilton, Andrew Puncher, Mathew Ollier, Daniel Walder, Daisy Houang, Anthony Petrilli, Joseph Mulcahy, Morag Morrison, Chris Bamborough, Robert Page, Nina Strunk, Nimi Attanayake, Marvin Chik.
Collaborators	Gardiner & Theobald LLP (Cost Consultant) Adams Kara Taylor (Structural Engineer) Max Fordham LLP (Environmental Consultant) Grant Associates (Landscape Architects) Charcoalblue (Theatre Consultant) RBA Accoustics (Acoustic Consultants) NK Projects (Artist) SEA Design (Graphics and Branding)

062\
Stratford Regional Station

Location	London Borough of Newham, UK
Client	Network Rail/ ODA / London Underground / Jacobs
Value	£65m
Date	Completion 2010
Project Team	Roger Hawkins, Russell Brown, Morag Morrison, Harbinder Birdi, Robert Page, Peter van der Zwan, Donna Walker, Nick Gaskell, Ida Hess, Ann Kristin Jeetun, Patrick Drewello, Anna MacDougall, Daisy Houang, Alex Smith, Michael Paris, Marvin Chik.
Collaborators	Jacobs Engineering (Lead Consultant) Arup Acoustics (Acoustic Engineer) Piniger and Partners (Lighting) Schuman Smith (Specification Writing) London Underground (User Client) Network Rail (Construction Manager, User Client, Project Manager) TfL (Funding Client) Olympic Delivery Authority (Present Funding Client) Tubelines (Contractor for London Underground) Metronet (Tracks Contractor) Morgan EST (Contractor for London Underground Assets) Browes Bion (Signage Designer for TFL) Hochtief (Contractor for Network Rail Assets) E.C. Harris (Previous Quantity Surveyor) Adams Henry (Planning Consultant) Massimo (CGI) Network Model Makers (Model Maker)

066\
Dubai Arts Pavilion

Location	Al Khor Park, Dubai, United Arab Emirates
Client	Arts and Cultural Office, Dubai
Value	£40m
Date	Completion 2010
Size	10,000 m²
Project Team	Roger Hawkins, Russell Brown, David Bickle, Darryl Chen, Nick Gaskell, Robert Page, Nina Strunk, Rebecca Williams, Anna MacDougall.
Collaborators	OMA (Masterplan Architect) Rock Hunter (CGI Studio) Arup Associates (Structure and Services)

070\
Massar Children's Discovery Centre

Location	Damascus, Syria
Client	Massar
Value	$57m
Date	Competition 2006 – runner up
Size	14,000 m²
Project Team	Roger Hawkins, Russell Brown, David Bickle, Euan MacDonald, Alex Smith, Nick Gaskell, Daisy Houang, Mike McLeod, Andrea Schrader.
Collaborators	ARUP (Environmental Engineer) A Models (Model Makers)

072\
Tottenham Court Road, Crossrail Station

Location	City of Westminster, London, UK
Client	Crossrail /Arup
Value	£700m
Date	Completion 2016
Project Team	Roger Hawkins, Russell Brown, David Bickle, Harbinder Birdi, Seth Rutt, Katya Chikaher, Antony Davis, Claire Smith, Andrew Payne, Alex Bennett, Ann Kristin Jeetun, Janinder Bhatti, Marvin Chik, Peter van der Zwan.
Collaborators	Daniel Buren (Artist) Tamsin Dillon (Art on the Underground) Atkins (Civil Engineer) Arup (Structure, Services and Lighting)

076\
Dublin Metro North

Location	Dublin, Ireland
Client	Railway Procurement Agency
Value	£2.4billion
Date	Stage C 2006
Project Team	Roger Hawkins, Russell Brown, Harbinder Birdi, Antony Davis, Katya Chikaher, Alex Smith.
Collaborators	Jacobs (Structural, Services and Civil Engineer), Mccullough Mulvin Architects (Public Realm Architects)

078\
School of Arts

Location	University of Kent, Canterbury, UK
Client	University of Kent
Value	£6m
Date	Completion 2009
Size	2,900 m²
Contract	Design and build
Project Team	Roger Hawkins, Russell Brown, David Bickle, Emma Smart, Hazel York, Mathew Mallon, Carol Lees, Amita Kulkarni, Renata Sa, Luis Rojano, Ida Hess, Morag Morrison, Ruth Milne, Alexander Flash, Anand Sagoo, Chloe Sharpe, Angelique Wisse.
Collaborators	Arup (Services, Structural, Acoustic and Fire Engineers) Dearle and Henderson (Project Managers) Betteridge and Milsom (Employer's Agent) Northcroft (Quantity Surveyors) Farrer Huxley (Landscape Architects) CMA Planning (Planning Consultants) All Profiles (CDM Coordinator) SEA (Graphics / Signage) Rock Hunter (Visualisation) Morgan Ashurst (Contractor) RH Partnership (Contractor's Architect)

082\
Taipei Performing Arts Centre

Location	Taipei, Taiwan
Client	City of Taipei
Value	£70m
Date	Competition entry 2008
Size	40,000 m²
Project Team	Roger Hawkins, Russell Brown, David Bickle, Seth Rutt, Marvin Chik, Joseph Haire, Mark Sciberras, Zoe Hayes, Greg Moss.
Collaborators	Theatre Projects (Theatre Consultant) Arup Associates (Structure and Services) Rock Hunter (CGI Studio) Hanna Werning (Artist)

096\
The New Art Exchange

Location	Nottingham, UK
Client	New Art Exchange
Value	£3m
Date	Completion 2008
Size	1,500 m²
Contract	Traditional JCT98
Project Team	Roger Hawkins, Russell Brown, David Bickle, Harbinder Birdi, Seamus Lennon, Katya Chikaher, Mathew Mallon.
Collaborators	Hew Locke (Artist)
	Hetain Patel (Artist)
	Watermans Group (Services Engineers)
	Price & Myers (Structural Engineers)
	Focus (Project Manager)
	Davis Langdon (Quantity Surveyor)
Awards	Civic Trust Award 2009
	Nottingham Civic Society Commendation 2008
	RIBA Award 2009
	RIBA East Midlands Award 2009
	Nottingham Lord Mayor's Awards for Urban Design 2009 – Overall Award
	Nottingham Lord Mayor's Awards for Urban Design 2009 – New Build Award

102\
The Roald Dahl Museum and Story Centre

Location	Great Missenden, Buckinghamshire, UK
Client	Trustees of The Roald Dahl Museum and Story Centre
Value	£2m
Date	Completion 2005
Size	1,200 m²
Contract	Traditional, JCT98
Project Team	Roger Hawkins, Russell Brown, David Bickle, Seth Rutt, Anna MacDougall, Jeremy Walker, Wayne Glaze.
Collaborators	Bremner & Orr (Exhibition Designer)
	Price & Myers (Structural Engineers)
	Michael Popper Associates (Services Engineers)
	Appleyard & Trew (Quantity Surveyor / Planning Supervisor)
	Adrienne Hill (Planning Consultant)
Awards	British Guild of Travel Writers' Award 2006
	Civic Trust Award 2007
	Best UK Tourism Project
	Enjoy England Award for Excellence 2008 – Best Small Visitor Attraction

106\
Wysing Arts Centre

Location	Bourn, Cambridgeshire, UK
Client	Wysing Arts Trust
Value	£1.5m
Date	Completion 2008
Size	700 m²
Contract	Traditional, JCT 2005
Project Team	Roger Hawkins, Russell Brown, David Bickle, Jason Martin, Teresa Telander, Seamus Lennon, Sonya Flynn, Tanya Brown, Stephanie Schultze Westrum.
Collaborators	Haskin Robinson Waters (Structural Engineer)
	Max Fordham (Service Engineer)
	Stace Consulting (QS)
	WSG Jackson (Contractor)
Awards	RIBA Award 2008

112\
Fourth Plinth Proposal

Location	Trafalgar Square, Westminster, London, UK
Client	GLA
Date	2008
Project Team	Roger Hawkins, Russell Brown, David Bickle.
Collaborators	Bob and Roberta Smith (Artist)
	A Models (Model Makers)

116\
Tottenham Court Road Station Upgrade

Location	Camden\Westminster, London, UK
Client	Halcrow/LUL Ltd
Value	£280m
Date	Completion 2016
Contract	NEC 3 target cost
Project Team	Roger Hawkins, Russell Brown, Harbinder Birdi, Antony Davis, Mathew Mallon, Renata Sa, Patrick Drewello, Mark Edmond, Katya Chikaher, Claire Smith, Zoe Hayes. Janinder Bhatti, Morag Morrison, Seth Rutt, James Gosling, Jonathan Rush, Andrew Hamilton, David Kohn, Wayne Glaze, Marvin Chik, Peter van der Zwan, Michael Paris, Sonya Flynn, Alun Hughes, Rebecca Palmer, David Watkins, David Bertenshaw, Val Erdos, Giles Vallis, Julia Roberts, Emma Gerrard.
Collaborators	Daniel Buren (Artist)
	Tamsin Dillon (Art on the Underground)
	Halcrow (Structural Engineers)
	Acanthus LW (Station Architects)
	Stanton Williams (Plaza Entrance Architects)
	Gillespies (Landscape Architects)
	Adams Kara Taylor (Structural Engineers)
	Halcrow (Services Engineers)
	Pinniger & Partners (Lighting Design)
	FXV (CGI Studio)
	GMJ (CGI Studio)
	GVA Grimley (Planning Consultant)
	Montagu Evans (Planning Consultant)

120\
The Henry Moore Foundation, Sheep Field Barn Gallery

Location	Perry Green, Hertfordshire, UK
Client	The Henry Moore Foundation
Value	£0.5m
Date	Completion 1999
Size	400 m²
Contract	Traditional/IFC 98
Project Team	Roger Hawkins, Russell Brown, David Bickle, Seth Rutt, Andrew Groarke, Nicola Chambers.
Collaborators	Price & Myers (Structural Engineers)
	Michael Popper Associates (Services Engineers)

120\
The Henry Moore Foundation, Dane Tree House

Location	Perry Green, Hertfordshire, UK
Client	The Henry Moore Foundation
Value	£0.75m
Date	Project 1 – Completion 1998
	Project 2 – Completion 2002
Project Team	Roger Hawkins, Russell Brown, David Bickle, Seth Rutt.
Collaborators	Project 1 –
	Price & Myers (Structural Engineers)
	Michael Popper Associates (Services Engineers)
	Project 2 –
	Price & Myers (Structural Engineers)
	Atelier Ten (Services Engineers)
	Boyden & Co (Quantity Surveyor)

122\
Artists Studio and Apartment

Location	Tower Hamlets, London, UK
Client	Rachel Whiteread & Marcus Taylor
Value	£0.75m
Date	Completion 2002
Size	2,000 m²
Contract	JCT IFC
Project Team	Roger Hawkins, Russell Brown, David Bickle, Jason Martin, Hazel York, Greg Moss.
Collaborators	Barton Engineers Ltd (Structural)
	Boyden and Co (QS)
	Atelier Ten (Services Engineers)

132\
Wellesley Road and Park Lane Masterplan

Location — Croydon, London, UK
Client — Croydon Council
Value — £40m
Date — 2008 – ongoing
Size — 4.5 ha/1.5 linear km
Project Team — Roger Hawkins, Russell Brown, David Bickle, David Lomax,
Daniel Burn, Katie Tonkinson, Darryl Chen.
Collaborators — Squint Opera (Filmmakers)
Grant Associates (Landscape)
Glasgow School of Art Advanced Textiles Dept. (Scarf Printing)
Sally Spencer-Davies, (A Models)
Jason Bruges Studio (Lighting)
Hyder (Traffic Consultancy)
EC Harris (Cost Consultancy)

136\
70, St Johns Street

Location — 70 St Johns Street, Islington, London, UK
Client — SEA Design
Date — 2008 – ongoing
Size — 300 m²
Project Team — Roger Hawkins, Russell Brown, David Bickle, Mathew Ollier,
Emily Lawley, Alex Smith.
Collaborators — SEA Design

138\
OQO

Location — Islington, London, UK
Client — Capa Concept trading as OQO
Value — £300,000
Date — Completion 2005
Size — 300 m²
Contract — Design and build
Project Team — Roger Hawkins, Russell Brown, Jeremy Walker.
Collaborators — SEA Design (Branding)

140\
Scin

Location — Notting Hill, London, UK
Client — Scin Ltd
Value — £300,000
Date — Completion 2005
Size — 200 m²
Contract — Traditional, JCT Minor Works 98
Project Team — Roger Hawkins, Russell Brown, John Turner, Ida Hess.
Collaborators — SEA Design (Branding)
Packman Lucas (Structural Engineer)

142\
Metropolitan Wharf

Location — Tower Hamlets, London, UK
Client — Capital & Counties, Great Capital Partnership and
UK Real Estate.
Value — £6m
Date — Completion 2008
Size — 15,979 m²
Contract — Traditional JCT 98
Project Team — Roger Hawkins, Russell Brown, David Bickle, Katie Tonkinson,
Nick Rees, Alice Cutter, Beth Kay, Nimi Attanayake,
Laura Miller, Mathew Mallon, Angelique Wisse,
Clodagh McCallig.
Collaborators — SEA Design (Signage)
NRM (Structural Engineers)
Price & Myers (Structural Engineers)
Hurley Palmer Flatt (Services Engineers)
Barton Willmore (Planning Consultants)
CMA (Planning Consultants)
The Menzies Partnership (Fire Safety)
KM Heritage (Heritage Consultant)
Anstey Horne (Sunlight/Daylight Consultant)
Pilcher Hershman (Commercial Agent)

156\
Student Enterprise Building

Location — Coventry University, UK
Client — Coventry University
Value — £24m
Date — Completion 2011
Size — 8,500 m²
Contract — Design and build
Project Team — Roger Hawkins, Russell Brown, Morag Morrison, Neena Thakkar.
Antony Petrilli, Heidi Corbet, Nick Gaskell, Jason Martin,
Emily Pang, Marvin Chik, Alex Smith, Rebecca Williams,
Nina Strunk, Seth Rutt, Kim Winston, Angelique Wisse,
Chloe Sharpe, Ida Hess, Mathew Mallon, Alice Cutter.
Collaborators — Max Fordham (Services Engineers)
Adams Kara Taylor (Structural Engineers)
Davis Langdon (Project Manager)
Plincke (Landscape)
Gardiner & Theobold (Quantity Surveyor)
Rock Hunter (Visualisation)
A Models (Model Makers)

162\
The Terrace

Location — Tooley Street, Southwark, London, UK
Client — More London
Value — £6.4m
Date — Completion 2008
Size — 3,000 m²
Contract — JCT Traditional
Project Team — Roger Hawkins, Russell Brown, David Bickle, Carol Lees,
Anthony Petrilli, Jessica Billam, Chloe Sharpe, Emma Gerrard,
Jonathan Rush, Mathew Mallon.
Collaborators — Adams Kara Taylor (Structural Engineer)
RHB Partnership LLP (Services Engineer)
EC Harris (Cost Consultant)
Haymills Ltd (Contractors)
Arup (Masterplan)
Spears and Major Associates (Lighting Consultant)
Centre for Accessible Environments (Access / Disability
Consultant)
Townshend Landscape (Landscape Architect)
DP9 (Planning Consultant)

166\
Parliament Square

Location — Westminster, London, UK
Client — Transport for London
Value — £18m
Date — Placed on hold in 2008
Project Team — Roger Hawkins, Russell Brown, Antony Petrilli,
Anna MacDougall, Kim Winston, Matthew Ollier, Darryl Chen,
Carol Lees.
Collaborators — Vogt (Landscape Architects)
EDAW (Landscape Architects)
DSDHA (Consultant Urban Designer)
David Bonnett Associates & Centre For Accessible Environments
(Access Consultants)
Colin Buchanan (Traffic/Highways Consultant)
Montagu Evans (Planning and Conservation Consultant)
Jason Bruges Studio (Lighting Consultant)
Intelligent Space (Pedestrian Movement Consultants)
Awards — Westminster Society Special Award for outstanding work
in Design Development 2008

172\
New Faculty of Business and Law

Location — Kingston University, Kingston Hill Campus, London, UK
Client — Mace, Kingston University
Value — £25m
Date — Planning consent Feb 2009
Completion summer 2011
Size — 7,200 m²
Project Team — Roger Hawkins, Russell Brown, Nicola Rutt, Petr Kalab,
Neena Thakkar, David Lomax, Donna Walker.
Collaborators — Mace Ltd (Project Manager)
Sense (Cost Consultant)
Hurley Palmer Flatt (Mechanical and Electrical Engineering)
Scott Wilson (Structural Engineering)

176\
New Biochemistry

Location	University of Oxford Science Area, Oxford, UK
Client	Oxford University Estates
Value	£50m (Phase 1), £65m (Phase 2)
Date	Completion 2008
Size	12,000 m² (Phase 1)
Contract	Two stage design and build
Project Team	Roger Hawkins, Russell Brown, David Bickle, Oliver Milton, Hazel York, Morag Morrison, Mathew Mallon, Anthony Petrilli, Louisa Bowles, Emma Smart, Greg Moss, Ida Hess, Michael Hammock, Robert Corser, Angelique Wisse, Anna Carlquist, Anand Sagoo, Chloe Sharpe.
Collaborators	Nicky Hirst, Tim Head, Annie Catrell, Peter Fraser (Artists) Laing O'Rourke (Contractor) pdcm, (Project Manager) Crown House (Services Contractor) Peter Brett Associates (Structural Engineer) Foreman Roberts (Services Engineer) Turner and Townsend (Quantity Surveyor)
Awards	RIBA Award 2009 Structural Steel Design Award 2009 World Architecture Festival Award 2009 – shortlisted

176\
Clarendon Laboratory Annexe (Theoretical and Experimental Physics)

Location	University of Oxford Science Area, Oxford, UK
Client	University of Oxford
Value	£30m
Date	Planning 2010, completion 2012
Size	5,000 m²
Contract	Two stage design and build
Project Team	Roger Hawkins, Russell Brown, Oliver Milton, Euan MacDonald, Louisa Bowles, Mathew Ollier, Joseph Mackey, Chloe Sharpe, Lucy Dinnen.
Collaborators	Price & Myers (Structural Engineer) Silcock Dawson (Services Engineer) EC Harris (Cost Consultant) Heery International (Project Manager) DPDS (Planning Consultant)

176\
Department of International Development, Queen Elizabeth House

Location	Mansfield Road, Oxford, UK
Client	Oxford University Estates
Value	£3m
Date	Completion 2009
Size	1,000 m²
Contract	Two Stage Traditional, JCT98
Project Team	Roger Hawkins, Russell Brown, Oliver Milton, Hazel York, Louisa Bowles, Peter Wraight, Chloe Sharpe, Mathew Mallon, William Newell.
Collaborators	Longcross (Contractor) Confluence CPM (Project Manager) Giffords (Structural Engineer) Hoare Lea (Services Engineer)

176\
Relocated Jericho Health Centre

Location	University of Oxford, UK
Client	Oxford University Estates
Value	£10m
Date	Projected completion 2010
Size	4,000 m²
Contract	Two stage design and build
Project Team	Roger Hawkins, Russell Brown, Oliver Milton, Carol Lees, Anna Pamphilion, Joseph Mackey, Daniel Burn, Josephine Glyn, Anand Sagoo.
Collaborators	Niall McLaughlan Architects (Masterplan Architect) Pell Frischmann (Structural Engineer) Hoare Lea (Services Engineer) Gardiner & Theobald (Cost Consultant) RB Development Management (Project Manager) Turnberry Consulting (Planning Consultant)

176\
Department of Engineering Science, Thom Building

Location	University of Oxford, UK
Client	Oxford University Estates
Value	£15m
Date	Projected completion 2011
Size	6,500 m²
Contract	Two stage design and build
Project Team	Roger Hawkins, Russell Brown, Oliver Milton, Anna MacDougall, Matthew Ollier, Joseph Haire.
Collaborators	Turner & Townsend (Cost Consultant) AKS Ward (Structural Engineer) Silcock Dawson & Partners (Services Engineer) DPDS (Planning Consultant) Newtecnic (Cladding Consultant) PDCM (Project Managers)

184\
Gillett Square

Location	Hackney, London, UK
Client	Hackney Co-Operative Developments/ SRB Haggerston/ ERDF/ Groundwork Hackney/ MacDonald Egan
Value	£18m
Date	Phase 1 Completion 1997 - Bradbury Street Workshops Phase 2 Completion 1999 – Market Stalls Phase 3 Completion 2004 – Culture House Phase 4 Planning 2004 – ongoing, Stamford Works Phase 5 Completion 2007 – Gillett Square
Project Team	Roger Hawkins, Russell Brown, David Bickle, Wayne Glaze, Beth Kay, Antony Petrilli, Andrew Puncher, David Money, Vicky Emmett.
Awards	Architects' Journal Small Projects Award 2000 Design Week Best Retail Environment Award 2001 Civic Trust Award – Mention 2002

194\
Selected Projects

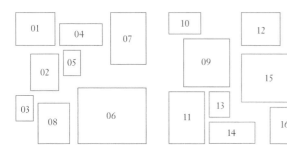

01 42-44 Beak Street, Soho, London, UK, 1988 – 1990
02 25 Lisle Street, Soho, London, UK, 1988 – 1990
03 33 Old Bond Street, Mayfair, London UK, 1989 – 1991
04 PlayBarn and PlayArc, Newham, London, UK, 1988 – 1989
05 Dane Tree House, The Henry Moore Foundation, Perry Green,
   Hertfordshire, UK, 1991 – 1993
06 227 Wood Lane, London, Women's Pioneer Housing, White City,
   UK, 1993 – 1995

07 Avenue Campus Faculty of Arts, University of Southampton,
   UK, 1993 – 1996
08 St Mary Square, Bury St Edmunds, UK, 1994 – 1998
09 Birmingham Institute of Art & Design, Gosta Green Campus,
   University of Central England, UK, 1994 – 1996
10 Bradbury Street Workshops, Hackney, London, UK, 1994 – 1995
11 Community Resource Centre, Major Road, Newham, London,
   UK, 1993 – 1994

12 Sheep Field Barn Gallery, The Henry Moore Foundation,
   Perry Green, Hertfordshire, UK, 1997 – 1999
13 Students Union, Queen Mary, University of London, Tower Hamlets,
   UK, 1996 – 1999
14 School Refurbishment & Extension, Herts & Essex High School,
   Bishops Stortford, UK, 1996 – 1998
15 Hope Sufferance Wharf, Southwark, London, UK, 1994 – 1997
16 Trowbridge Centre for Adults with Learning Disabilities, Hackney,
   London, UK, 1997 – 2000

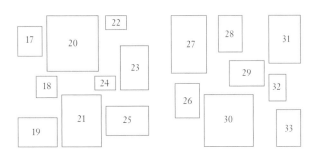

17 Market Stalls, Gillett Square, London, UK, 1998 – 1999
18 Tottenham Court Road Station Upgrade, London, UK,
    1998 – ongoing
19 The Oakwood Centre, Woodley, Berkshire, UK, 1996 – 1999
20 Hawkins\Brown Studio, 60 Bastwick Street, London, UK, 1998
21 New Student Union, University of Portsmouth, UK, 2000 – 2002

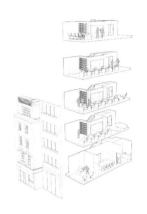

22 Artists Studio and Apartment, Bethnal Green Road, Tower Hamlets, London, UK, 2000 – 2002
23 91-93 Farringdon Road, Islington, London, UK, 2001 – 2002
24 GreenPoint, Edgware Road, Barnet, London, UK, 2001 – ongoing
25 The Roald Dahl Museum and Story Centre, Great Missenden, Buckinghamshire, UK, 2001 – 2005
26 The Culture House, Hackney, London, UK, 2001 – 2004

27 The Terrace, Tooley Street, Southwark, London, UK, 2000 – 2008
28 70 St Johns Street, Islington, London, UK, 2007 – ongoing
29 Maggie's Cancer Care Centre, Sheffield, UK, 2001 – 2002
30 Anglia Ruskin University, Cambridge, UK, 2002 – 2004
31 Dagenham Town Hall, Essex, UK, 2001 – 2003
32 Westminster Bridge Road, Southwark, London, UK, 2002 – ongoing
33 St Johns Path, Clerkenwell, London, UK, 2002 – 2004

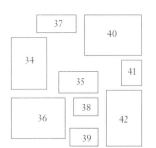

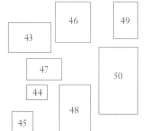

34 Barking Town Hall, Essex, UK, 2003 – 2006
35 Central Park Play Building, Newham, London, UK, 2003 – 2005
36 Culverin Court & Mount Carmel School, Islington,
   London, UK, 2003 – 2006
37 Thomas Danby Community Campus, Leeds, UK, 2003 – 2006
38 Poplar High Street, Tower Hamlets, London, UK, 2004 – 2009
39 Outlook Buildings, Shoeburyness, Essex, UK, 2003 – 2006

40 Wysing Arts Centre, Bourn, Cambridgeshire, UK 2004 – 2008
41 OQO, Islington, London, UK, 2004 – 2005
42 **New Biochemistry, University of Oxford, UK, 2004 – 2008**
43 **The New Art Exchange, Nottingham, UK, 2004 – 2008**
44 The Bottle Store, Stockwell Green, London, UK, 2004 – 2006
45 Boscombe Housing & Library, Bournemouth, UK, 2005 – 2007

46 Corby Cube, Northamptonshire, UK, 2005 – ongoing
47 Social Science Research Centre, University of Essex, Colchester, UK, 2004 – 2006
48 Parkhill, Sheffield, UK, 2006 – ongoing
49 Scin, Notting Hill, London, UK, 2004 – 2005
50 2 Hillman Street, Hackney, London UK, 2004 – 2008

200

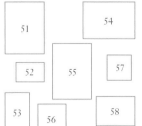
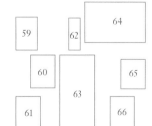

51 Yavneh College, Enfield, London, UK, 2006 – 2009
52 Stoke Newington Town Hall & Assembly Hall, Hackney, London, UK, 2005 – 2010
53 Wharf Road, Hackney, London, UK, 2005 – 2008
54 Metropolitan Wharf, Tower Hamlets, London, UK, 2005 – 2008
55 Highfields Automotive & Engineering Centre, Nottingham Science Park, UK, 2005 – 2008

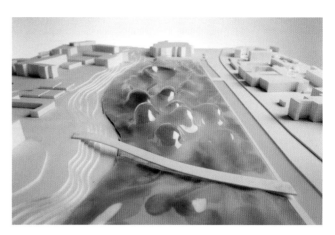

56 Clarendon Laboratory Annexe (Theoretical and Experimental
   Physics), University of Oxford, UK, 2009 – ongoing
57 The Wharves, Deptford, London, UK, 2006 – ongoing
58 Stratford Regional Station, London, UK, 2005 – 2010
59 All Saints Community Centre, New Cross, London, UK, 2006 – 2009
60 School of Arts, University of Kent, Canterbury, UK, 2006 – 2010
61 Department of International Development, Queen Elizabeth House,

Oxford, UK, 2006 – 2009
62 Dublin Metro North, Dublin, Ireland, 2006 – ongoing
63 Fourth Plinth Proposal, Trafalgar Square, Westminster,
   London, UK, 2008
64 Massar Children's Discovery Centre, Damascus, Syria, 2006
65 Parliament Square, Westminster, London, UK, 2007 – 2008
66 Sevenstone New Retail Quarter, Sheffield, UK, 2007 – ongoing

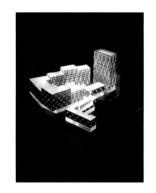

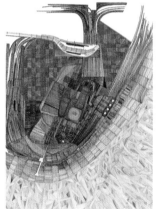

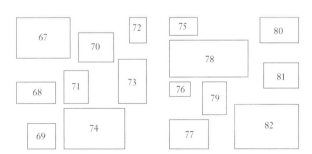

```
┌──────┐                  ┌──┐   ┌──┐          ┌──────┐
│  67  │              ┌──┐│72│   │75│      │  80  │
└──────┘          ┌──┐│70│└──┘   └──┘      └──────┘
              ┌──┐│70│              ┌────────────┐
              │70│└──┘              │     78     │
┌──────┐ ┌──┐ ┌──┐               └────────────┘  ┌──────┐
│  68  │ │71│ │73│            ┌──┐              │  81  │
└──────┘ └──┘ └──┘            │76│  ┌──┐        └──────┘
    ┌──────────┐              └──┘  │79│
┌──┐│    74    │          ┌──────┐  └──┘  ┌────────┐
│69│└──────────┘          │  77  │        │   82   │
└──┘                      └──────┘        └────────┘
```

67 Barking Town Hall Extension, Essex, UK, 2007
68 Chichester College Redevelopment, West Sussex, UK, 2007 – 2009
69 Clapham Estate, London, UK, 2008 – ongoing
70 Dubai Arts Pavilion, Al Khor Park, Dubai, UAE, 2007 – 2008
71 Pembury Circus, Hackney, London, UK, 2008
72 Brinsbury Campus Redevelopment, Chichester College,
   West Sussex, UK, 2008 – 2009

73 Shoeburyness Masterplan, Essex, UK, 2007 – 2008
74 Daventry I-Hub, Daventry Northamptonshire, UK, 2008
75 Student Enterprise Building, Coventry University, UK,
   2008 – 2011
76 New Faculty of Business and Law, Kingston University,
   London, UK, 2008 – 2011
77 Roussillon Barracks, Chichester, UK, 2008 – ongoing

78 My Place Youth Centre, Plashet Park, Newham, London, UK,
   2009 – ongoing
79 Department of Engineering Science, Thom Building, University
   of Oxford, UK, 2008 – ongoing
80 Taipei Performing Arts Centre, Taipei, Taiwan, 2008
81 Canada Water Regeneration, London, UK, 2008 – 2010
82 The Britten Pears Foundation, The Red House, Aldeburgh, UK, 2008

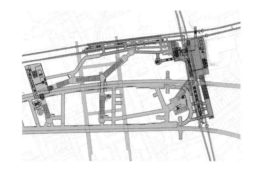

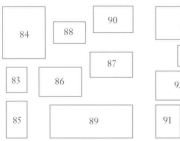

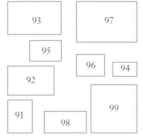

```
┌──────┐      ┌────┐  ┌────────┐      ┌──────────┐      ┌────────┐
│  84  │      │ 88 │  │   90   │      │    93    │      │   97   │
└──────┘      └────┘  └────────┘      └──────────┘      └────────┘
                         ┌────────┐       ┌────┐
                         │   87   │       │ 95 │    ┌────┐  ┌────┐
┌────┐  ┌────────┐       └────────┘       └────┘    │ 96 │  │ 94 │
│ 83 │  │   86   │                      ┌────────┐  └────┘  └────┘
└────┘  └────────┘                      │   92   │
                                        └────────┘
┌────┐  ┌──────────────┐   ┌────┐    ┌──────┐    ┌────────┐
│ 85 │  │      89      │   │ 91 │    │  98  │    │   99   │
└────┘  └──────────────┘   └────┘    └──────┘    └────────┘
```

83 Barking Abbey Masterplan, Barking, Essex, UK, 2009 – ongoing
84 Derby Moor Community Sports College, Derby, East Midlands,
   UK, 2009 – ongoing
85 Wellesley Road and Park Lane Design Competition, Croydon,
   London, UK, 2009
86 Tottenham Court Road, Crossrail Station, London, UK,
   2009 – ongoing
87 Abbey Green, Barking, Essex, UK, 2009

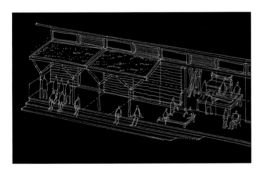

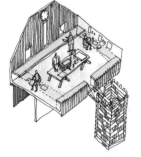

88 Emmanuel Primary School, Camden, London, UK, 2009 – ongoing
89 Woodberry Down, Oakend & Shops, Hackney, London,
   UK, 2009 – ongoing
90 Student Accommodation, Royal Veterinary College, Hatfield,
   Hertfordshire, UK, 2009 – ongoing
91 Oily Cart Offices, Tooting, Greater London, UK, 2009
92 Aldingbourne Country Centre, Chichester, West Sussex,
   UK, 2008 – 2009

93 31 Borough High Street, London, UK, 2009 – ongoing
94 East Croydon Masterplan, London, UK, 2009 – ongoing
95 Aston University Masterplan, Birmingham, UK, 2009 – ongoing
96 Woodberry Down, Horston and Sherwood, Hackney,
   London, UK, 2010 – ongoing
97 Islington Housing Design Competition, London, UK, 2009
98 The Magnet, Oxford, UK, 2009
99 Lower Marsh Street Regeneration, Southwark, UK, London, 2010

Biographies

Tim Abrahams is Associate Editor of the architecture and design magazine *Blueprint*. His areas of expertise are technical innovation in design, the re-use of significant buildings and city-making. He also writes about architecture and urbanism for *Wired*.

Jes Fernie is a freelance curator and writer. Her book *Two Minds, Artists and Architects in Collaboration* was published by Black Dog Publishing in 2006. She curates lecture programmes, edits books and writes for the art and architecture press. She also works with architectural practices and galleries on commissioning programmes for the public realm, most recently with first site for a major temporary sculpture in Jaywick, Essex by Nathan Coley and with the Tate and Serpentine Gallery for a research project related to 2012. In her role as Associate for Art in the Open, she is a member of the Olympic Delivery Authority's art commissioning panels as well as Design for London's Great Spaces scheme. She has collaborated with Hawkins\Brown on a number of projects since 2005.

Adam Hart is a social scientist, bricklayer and musician educated at Oxford, Cambridge and Sussex Universities, the London School of Film Technique and the Dudley Skill Centre. He has lived mostly in Hackney since graduating in 1966 except for some ten years on a canal boat in the Midlands. Amongst other occupations he has worked as a lorry driver, builder, community service organiser and as a social researcher at the Tavistock Institute of Human Relations with young people leaving care. Since 1991 he has been able to put this skill set to best use for the community-based regeneration of Dalston working for Hackney Co-operative Developments as its executive director. He is based there with much of his family, when he is not in Cornwall or elsewhere.

Lee Mallett communicates ideas in the built environment. His company Urbik works with developers, architects and public sector agencies helping them explain urban regeneration projects. He publishes two newsletters and a magazine about planning in London. He is former editor of *Building Design* and *Property Week* and a steering group member of the London Festival of Architecture, and co-chair of My City Too! – an Open City campaign to give young people a voice in improving London's public realm.

Vicky Richardson is director of architecture, design and fashion at the British Council. Previously she was editor of *Blueprint*, the UK's leading magazine of architecture and design. Under her editorship (2004–2010) *Blueprint* was relaunched to critical acclaim and won many awards for its design and content. Vicky is a regular public speaker and chair of architecture and design events, and has been a jury member for many high-profile design competitions. She is a member of the London Mayor's Cultural Strategy Group and a trustee of the educational charity, The Campaign for Drawing. Vicky has a degree in architecture from the University of Westminster. She also studied fine art at Chelsea School of Art and Central St Martins. She has written several books, including *In Defence of the Dome* (ASI, 1999) and *New Vernacular Architecture* (Laurence King, 2002).

Adam Ritchie is a partner at Max Fordham LLP (Engineering, Design, Environment) and leads the practice's sustainable urban design group. He is the editor of *Sustainable Urban Design. An Environmental Approach* (Taylor and Francis, 2009) and co-authored *Environmental Design* (Spon Press, 2003). Adam is in charge of the MEP engineering team developing the design of the Zero-Carbon Masdar Institute Neighbourhood in Abu Dhabi.

Erik Spiekermann is an information architect, type designer and author of books and articles on type and typography. He was founder of MetaDesign (1979), Germany's largest design firm working for clients such as Audi, Skoda, Volkswagen, Berlin Transit and Düsseldorf Airport. In 1988 he started FontShop, a company for production and distribution of electronic fonts. He has redesigned *The Economist* magazine in London, written a book called *Stop Stealing Sheep* (Adobe Press) and created a corporate font family for Nokia. In May 2007 he was the first designer to be elected into the Hall of Fame by the European Design Awards for Communication Design. Erik is Honorary Professor at the University of the Arts in Bremen and in 2006 received an honorary doctorship from Pasadena Art Center. He was made an Honorary Royal Designer for Industry by the RSA in Britain in 2007 and Ambassador for the European Year of Creativity and Innovation by the European Union for 2009. He now runs EdenSpiekermann with offices in Berlin and Amsterdam.

Staff 1988–2010
Present\Past

Robin Adamski
Karin Andres
Nimi Attanayake
Tessa Baird
Chris Bamborough
Natalie Beavis
Alexandria Beckett
Alexander Bennett
David Bertenshaw
Janinder Bhatti
David Bickle
Jessica Billam
Katherine Bird
Harbinder Birdi
Eva Boardman
Joseph Boniface
Sophie Bould
Louisa Bowles
Nick Brown
Russell Brown
Tanya Brown
Jasper Browne
Jonathan Buckland
Daniel Burn
Jacqueline Campbell
Anna Carlquist
Helen Carroll
Nicola Chambers
Darryl Chen
Marvin Chik
Katya Chikaher
Celia Christie
Iain Cochran
Heidi Corbet
Robert Corser
Jelena Cousins
Alice Cutter
Alan Davies
Antony Davis
Nick Digance
Lucy Dinnen
Jeremy Donaldson
Louise Donohoe
Simon Dove
Patrick Drewello
Mary Duggan
Natalie Dumont
Mark Edmond
Vicky Emmett
Val Erdos
Esther Everett
Cormac Farrelly
Aimee Felton
Stuart Finnie
Alex Flash
Sonya Flynn
Jane Foulkes
Steve Fox

Louise Freeman
Rebecca Fuge
Michael Garnett
Nick Gaskell
Jeremy Gay
Hannah Gaze
Emma Gerrard
Beth Giblenn
Wayne Glaze
Josephine Glyn
Andy Gollifer
Aimee Goodwin
James Gosling
Tom Graham
Jessica Gray
Russell Gray
Andrew Groarke
Caroline Habgood
Joseph Haire
Louise Hales
Georgina Hall
Chris Halpin
Andrew Hamilton
Michael Hammock
Björk Haraldsdóttir
Anna Hart
Roger Hawkins
Zoe Hayes
Myra Haywood
Tonya Hemburrow
Ida Mai Hess
Thomas Hillier
Leyla Hilmi
Nadine Holland
Tanya Holland
Alison Holroyd
Daisy Houang
Josef Huber
Alun Hughes
Elinor Hughes
Nicola Hughes
Gillian Hyndman
Ann Kristin Jeetun
Felicity Joll
Petr Kalab
Mayuko Kanasugi
Anne Kapoor
Preet Kapoor
Beth Kay
Kizzi Keane
David Kohn
Amita Kulkarni
Sarah Ladkani
Lucy Lavers
Emily Lawley
Rebecca Lee
Carol Lees
Seamus Lennon

Rebecca Lesser
Richard Lewis
Shane Lincoln
Justin Lomas
David Lomax
David Loughlin
Euan Macdonald
Anna MacDougall
Joseph Mackey
Michael Macleod
Peter Madsen
Asma Malik
Mathew Mallon
Caitlin Marks
Mark Marshall
Steve Marshall
Jason Martin
Paula Mason
Christian Matthies
Clodagh McCallig
Keil McConville
Mary McKenzie
Laura Mclean
Erna Mertens
Campbell Metcalfe
Laura Miller
Gavin Mills
Ruth Milne
Oliver Milton
Nicole Mokwe
David Money
Lucy Montgomery
Jamie Morris
Jonathan Morrison
Morag Morrison
Gregory Moss
Anna Motture
Joseph Mulcahy
Benjamin Newcomb
William Newell
Rentaro Nishimura
Tom O'Byrne
Aimee O'Carroll
Jennifer O'Donnell
Paul O'Keefe
Felix Oefelein
Matthew Ollier
Robert Page
Andrew Paine
Ivana Palesova
Rebecca Palmer
Anna Pamphilon
Emily Pang
Robin Panrucker
Michael Paris
Simon Parsons
Savan Patel
Sian Patterson

Anthony Petrilli
Christopher Phillips
Tommy Pniewski
Sofia Pomares Anton
Dor Pontin
John Proctor
Andrew Puncher
Nina Quesnell
Anne Rabbitt
Simon Reed
Nick Rees
Richard Rees
Julia Roberts
Frances Robertson
Kylie Robinson
Luis Rojano
Louise Rothwell
Jonathan Rush
Nicola Rutt
Seth Rutt
Renata Sa
Anand Sagoo
Lauren Saville
Andrea Schrader
Stephanie Schultze Westrum
Ulrike Schwickerath
Mark Sciberras
Punya Sehmi
Chloe Sharpe
Noriko Shimamura
Leonie Simms
Alexis Skeates
Emma Smart
Alex Smith
Claire Smith
Melanie Smith
Biba Smith-Fibiger
Sheila Sogbodjor
Gareth Stapleton
Jannie Steel
Myles Stinton
Sanna Stradling
Nina Strunk
Lisa Tanner
Paul Taylor
Raks Taylor
Teresa Telander
Ulla Tervo
Neena Thakkar
Katie Tonkinson
John Turner
Matthew Turner
Giles Vallis
Peter van der Zwan
Eva Vysoka
Daniel Walder
Donna Walker
Jeremy Walker

Stephen Ware
Tamsin Waterston
Andy Watts
Liss Werner
Paul Westwood
Claire White
Matthew White
Karen Willcox
John Williams
Melanie Williams
Rebecca Williams
Tom Williams
Adam Winstanley
Kim Winston
Angelique Wisse
Nicole Woodman
Peter Wraight
Hazel York
Stefan Zalewski

Illustration Credits

Animated Remedy. p203 middle right.

Binet, Hélène. p98, p107 top & bottom,
p108 top, bottom left & bottom right, p198 top right.

Bob & Roberta Smith. p113, p201 bottom middle.

Carter, Nick. p195 bottom middle.

Castillon, Santiago. p194 top middle, p195 bottom left.

Chesbo Photo. p143 top.

Chisnall, Matt. p184 bottom.

Clements, Daniel. p48, p50, p56, p60-61, p79 top & bottom,
p80 top left, top right & bottom, p201 middle left.

Collie, Keith. p16, p20, p92, p103 top & bottom, p104 top left & right,
bottom left & right, p126, p128, p141 all, p150, p196 top middle,
p196 bottom right, p197 top right, p197 bottom middle,
p198 middle middle, p198 middle left, p198 bottom middle & left,
p199 middle left & bottom left, p200 top left, p201 top left.

Crocker, Tim. p42 bottom, p43, p44 top right & bottom, p64-65 top,
p98 top & bottom left, p100, p143 bottom, p144, p145 middle & bottom,
p163, p164 bottom, p165 top & bottom, p176, p178, p180 all, p183,
p186 bottom, p187 top, p197 top left, p197 top right, p198 bottom right,
p199 top left & right, p199 bottom right, p200 top right,
p200 middle & left, p201 bottom left.

Eyelevel Creative Ltd. p37 top & bottom, p200 middle right.

FXV. p199 middle left below, p196 middle left.

Gardner, Gareth & The British Council. p14.

Gentile, Massimo. p65 bottom left & right, p198 middle below,
p202 top left.

Gilbert, Dennis / View. p121 all, p194 bottom right, p195 top right,
p196 bottom middle.

GMJ. p73 top & bottom, p170-171 top & bottom, p205 bottom middle.

Grant Associates. p134 top & bottom.

Gurak, Wojtek. p10, p41 top, bottom left & bottom right, p44 top left.

Gutteridge Nick. p200 bottom left.

Hirst, Nicky. p90.

Hobhouse, Jack. p26, p27, p37 top & bottom, p38, p66, p70 bottom,
p71 bottom, p133, p134 top right, p166, p169, p201 top right & middle
right, p202 top right, p203 bottom right, p204 bottom left.

Hufton, Nick / View. p195 bottom right.

Iddon, Henry. p198 top left.

IDFGlobal. p204 top right, p205 middle.

Kane, Nick. p196 middle right.

Keate, Andy & Ahlburg, Sussie. p195 middle right.

Locke, Hew. p99 bottom right.

Morris, Chris. p194 bottom middle, p194 middle middle,
p195 top left & below.

Morris, James. p194 top right.

New Tecnic. p203 middle middle.

Nicholson, David. p194 top left & middle left.

Palmer Cristobal. p148, p152, p185, p186 top.

Parker, Adam. p197 bottom left.

Peake, Nigel. p202 middle right.

Phipps, Simon. p139 top left & bottom, p198 middle right.

Putler, Andrew. p158 top & bottom, p202 bottom middle.

Rock Hunter Ltd. p27-28 top, p28 bottom, p29 top, middle & bottom,
p55, p57 top right, p68 top, p69, p83, p86-87, p157, p160-161,
p161 bottom, p182, p196 middle middle, p199 middle top,
p200 middle bottom, p202 middle top, p202 middle left, p203 right top,
p204 middle left, p205 top left, p205 bottom right.

Ross, John. p32 bottom, p34, p62, p200 bottom right, p201 bottom right.

SEA Design. p137 bottom left, p138 top, p139 top right, p14 top.

Spencer, Edmund. p195 middle middle.

Spencer-Davies, Sally. p112.

Staton, Sarah. p114, p115 top.

Studio Egret West. p205.

Studio Egret West, Grant Associates & Hawkins\Brown. p21.

SmithDog Photography. p36.

Smoothe. p22-23 top, p23 bottom, p25.

Squint/Opera. p33 top & bottom.

Tekuchi & Hawkins\Brown. p117 top.

Visualisation One. p204 bottom right, p204 top left.

All other images by Hawkins\Brown.

The authors and the publisher thank the photographers, architects and
organisations for the kind permission to reproduce the photographs
and illustrations in this book. Every effort has been made to trace
the copyright holders of images. We apologise in advance for any
unintentional omission and would be happy to insert the appropriate
acknowledgement in any subsequent edition of the book.